Edition KWV

Die „Edition KWV" beinhaltet hochwertige Werke aus dem Bereich der Wirtschaftswissenschaften. Alle Werke in der Reihe erschienen ursprünglich im Kölner Wissenschaftsverlag, dessen Programm Springer Gabler 2018 übernommen hat.

Weitere Bände in der Reihe http://www.springer.com/series/16033

Nadine Holtvogt

The Service Routing Problem

Modeling and Solution Approaches

Springer Gabler

Nadine Holtvogt
Wiesbaden, Germany

Bis 2018 erschien der Titel im Kölner Wissenschaftsverlag, Köln
Dissertation Universität zu Köln, 2011

Edition KWV
ISBN 978-3-658-24125-4 ISBN 978-3-658-24126-1 (eBook)
https://doi.org/10.1007/978-3-658-24126-1

Library of Congress Control Number: 2019933862

Springer Gabler

Originally published by Kölner Wissenschaftsverlag, Köln, 2011

This Springer Gabler imprint is published by the registered company Springer Fachmedien Wiesbaden GmbH part of Springer Nature
The registered company address is: Abraham-Lincoln-Str. 46, 65189 Wiesbaden, Germany

Acknowledgements

"To educate yourself for the feeling of gratitude means to take nothing for granted, but to always seek out and value the kind that will stand behind the action. Nothing that is done for you is a matter of course. Everything originates in a will for the good, which is directed at you. Train yourself never to put off the word or action for the expression of gratitude."

(Albert Schweitzer)

Writing a PhD thesis is a long journey with many hurdles and dead ends. Eventually, I reached the goal - the successful finalization of my PhD studies. The endless support and guidance of many people helped me to find the right path. All these people I owe a debt of gratitude.

First of all, I would like to thank my supervisor Prof. Ulrich Thonemann. He helped me to develop my personal and professional skills. The door to his office was always open to discuss my research questions. For his guidance and support I am honestly thankful. I would also like to thank Prof. Horst Tempelmeier for kindly co-supervising the thesis and Prof. Ludwig Kuntz for heading the thesis defense.

During my time as a PhD student, I met many people, namely Marc Albers, Michael Becker-Peth, Andreas Brinkhoff, Michael Decker, Nicola Decking, Marcus Dettenbach, André Fuetterer, Torsten Gully, Tanja Haeger, Moritz Heininger, Dominik Heinz, Katja Henne, Kai Hoberg, Simon Höller, Christina Jakobs, Sebastian Jucken, Silke Jütte, Kerstin Kubik, Anna Küpper, Philipp Laufenberg, Katharina Nachtsheim, Philipp Naujoks, Ulf Merschmann, Raik Özsen, Henning Olbert, Felix Papier, Vladislav Richter, Kathrin Rieger, Johanna Rosenbusch, Lisa Scheele, Frank Schneider, Jeanette Seifert, Marcel Sieke, Analena Stern, Carina von Weyhe, Alexander Weyers, and Jingnan Zhu. Besides working together and discussing research questions, we had many fun nights out together. Hence, I am really looking forward to the upcoming "Supply Chain Dinner" events.

Special thanks go to Anne Lange and Raik Özsen for proofreading and helping me to finalize my thesis. Anne Lange shared her own experiences in writing a PhD thesis and supported me by numerous helpful discussions.

However, I have to thank Raik Özsen not only for being a colleague, but for believing in me. I am grateful for his overwhelming support, for cheering me up, and for helping me to forget about the thesis when I needed a break.

Finally, I have to thank my family. Especially, I am deeply thankful for the support of my parents, Brigitte and Eduard. They were always there for me and encouraged me to make my dreams come true.

Cologne, 2011

Nadine Holtvogt

Contents

List of Figures

List of Tables

List of Algorithms

List of Abbreviations

AP	Assignment problem
BS	Benchmark solution
CPU	Central processing unit
K-SPP	K-th shortest path problem
LP	Linear program
LP-relaxation	Linear program relaxation
LRS	Local random search
MP	Master problem
MP_{IP}	Integer master problem
MCFP	Minimum cost flow problem
r-SAP	Shortest spanning r-arborescence problem
RMP	Restricted master problem
SA	Simulated annealing
SD	Steepest descent
SPP	Shortest path problem
SPPRC	Shortest path problem with resource constraints
TRACS	Trip pairing for airline crew scheduling

TRIP	Trip (re)-evaluation and improvement program
TS	Tabu search

List of Symbols

A	Set of arcs in a graph
a^*	Best found column in subproblem
A_n	Set of outgoing arcs of node n
a_{curr}	Arc connected to l_{curr}
a_{ij}	Decision variable, if duty j inculdes activity i
a_i^r	Lower bound for resource constraint of resource r at node i
a_j	Column j
α	Node in search tree of branch-and-bound approach
α'	Node in search tree of branch-and-bound approach
α''	Node in search tree of branch-and-bound approach
β_i	Demand and supply for node i
b_i^{end}	End of time window at customer i
b_i^{start}	Start of time window at customer i
b_i^r	Resource constraint of resource r at node i
b	Number of coverings
B_{ij}^{lower}	Lower bound representing the capacity constraints of arc (i,j)
B_{ij}^{upper}	Upper bound representing the capacity constraints of arc (i,j)

$c(P_i)$	Cost of path P_i
$C(\alpha)$	Set of all customers that are forbidden to be next on $P(\alpha)$
C_i	Reduced cost of a label at node i
$\bar{c}_{ij}$	Reduced cost for arc (i,j)
$\bar{c}$	Average labor plus transportation cost of filling a demand in the current planning period
c_b	Cost of benchmark solution
c_{ij}	Cost for traveling from i to j
$c(\tilde{\psi}(m,s,i^*(m,s)))$	Cost of best local shift of period s at site m
c_j	Cost of duty / column j
c_l	Labor cost
$cost_l$	Labor cost factor
$cost_t$	Travel cost factor
c_{over}	Penalty cost factor for one over-covering
c_p	Cost of path p
c_{refill}	Cost for refilling a tank
cr	Cooling rate
c_s	Service duty cost
$C_t(\theta,\varpi)$	Cost of period t with inventory policy θ and transportation policy ϖ
c_t	Travel cost
D_m^0	State of site m at the beginning of the planning horizon
D_m^H	State of site m at the end of the planning horizon
D_m^{max}	Upper bound for state at site m
d_i	Demand / usage rate
d	Destination / end node
$\Delta_{i^*(m,s),\psi}$	Difference between resulting cost $c(\tilde{\psi}(m,s,i^*(m,s)))$ and current minimum cost $c(\psi)$

$\Delta_{g',g}$	Change in objective function value by exchanging g by g'
Δ	Differences in the states at the beginning and end of the planning period
E	Earliest possible departure time from depot
end_i	End of service period of predecessor node i
$F(\alpha)$	Set of fixed tours with start and end at depot including node α
F	Tank size
$frac_{x_j}$	Fractional value of x_j in optimal solution of the restricted master problem
fr	Fraction of the sum of all fractional variable values
f	Non-negative and continuous function
$\nabla f(g)$	Gradient of $f(g)$
G	Graph
Γ	Latest possible arrival time at depot
g'	Solution for local and global search heuristics
g_0	Initial solution for local and global search heuristics
g_i	Solution of the i-th iteration of local and global search heuristics
g^*	Optimal solution of search heuristics
$\tilde{g}$	Solution for local and global search heuristics
g	Solution for local and global search heuristics
H	Planning horizon
h	Index for node, activity, duty, customer...

I_0	Opening / initial inventory
I	Set of all activities or tasks
i_B	Break node
it	Number of the current iteration
i_z	Node of a path with position z
i	Index for node, activity, duty, customer...
$i^*(m,s)$	Best local shift
$i^*_R(m,s)$	Best local shift to the right
$i^*_L(m,s)$	Best local shift to the left
J_i	Set of duties covering activity i
J_{new}	Set of new columns
j	Index for node, activity, duty, customer...
π	Non-negative vector of dual variables
J	Set of all possible and feasible duties
J'	Subset of feasible duties
J'_{left}	All columns of J'' that represents duties where delivery i is always after j or where neither delivery j nor i is covered
J''	Set of all generated columns for a branch
K	Index for K-th shortest path
$\bar{\kappa}$	Variable that allows to determine a lower bound for the optimal solution of the master problem
κ	Degree of a κ-degree center tree
k	Index for node, activity, duty, customer...
Λ	Set of all feasible solutions for local and global search heuristics
L_{Tabu}	Tabu list
l_h	Label number h

L_n	Set of labels for outgoing arcs of node n
$L(\psi)$	Set of service period and site combinations for table ψ
L	Set of labels
λ	Variable for evolutionary strategy based on Rechenberg (1973)
l_{curr}	Currend label to be examined
M	Set of sites
mk	Multiplication factor for CPU time limit for simulated annealing
μ	Generalized daily demand rate
m	Site
$N(g)$	Neighborhood of a solution g
NBS	Number of blocked iterations
N_B	Set of break nodes
N_D	Set of delivery nodes
N_{frac}	List of all fractional variable values
N	Set of nodes without depot
n_0	Number of iterations for determining the cost of the explored service periods during local random search
n_1	First randomly chosen node
n_{fix}	Number of fixed variables
n_{over}	Number of service deliverers that are over-covered
v	Vehicle
n	Number of all nodes in a graph or network, may be used for the number of cities, locations, sites, or customers
$\mathbb{N}_0$	Set of natural numbers including 0

$\mathbb{N}^+$	Set of natural numbers without 0
Ω	Set of all possible inventory policies
o	Origin / start node
$P(\alpha)$	Set of partial tours with start at depot associated with node α
$P(\Delta_{g',g},T)$	Probability function for exchanging g by g' depending on temperature T
Π	Set of all possible transportation policies
P_i	Path from the source node o to node i
$\bar{\pi}$	Dual variable of optimal solution of the restricted master problem
p_0	Acceptance probability after n_0 iterations
p_E	Acceptance probability after n_{SA} iterations
π_i	Dual variable that corresponds to service delivery i
pn	Predetermined number of columns with negative reduced cost to be chosen
$\tilde{\psi}(m,s,i)$	Service table resulting from shifting service period s of table ψ at site m by i periods
ψ	Service table
pv	Predetermined number of variables to be fixed
p	Path
Q	Capacity of a vehicle
q	Total load of a q-route
RO	Number of arcs for RO-opt algorithm index
$\mathbb{R}^n$	n-dimensional real number space
R	Set of resources that represent the constraints of the underlying problem

r	Resource
S	Subset of node set V
SC	Set of all columns
sd	Service delivery time
σ_{iv}	Starting time of vehicle v at node i
sl_i	Step length of iteration i
$start_j$	Starting time of service period at tail node j
s	Service period
T_0	Starting temperature
T_E	Temperature at the end of the period
Θ_i	Angle value for randomly chosen i
T_i^r	Accumulated consumption of resource r for a path from the origin o to node i
T_{it}	Temperature in iteration it
T	Temperature
t_0	CPU time until the local optimum is detected
τ	Predetermined value as lower bound for SCORE-value
θ	Vector representing inventory policy
t_{ij}^r	Resource consumption of arc (i,j) for resource r
t_{ij}	Travel time from i to j
$t(l_h)$	Travel time of path with label l_h to tail node
t_m^{max}	Latest possible time to deliver service
t_m	Latest service at site m
t_{SA}	CPU time limit for simulated annealing
t	Time period
Υ	Random number

u_i	Auxiliary variable for Miller-Tucker-Zemlin subtour elimination constraints
V	Set of nodes in a graph
VE	Fleet of vehicles
$v(S)$	Minimum number of arcs leaving customer subset S
ϖ	Vector representing transportation policy
w_{break}	Maximum work time without a break
w_j	Total work time of duty j
w_{max}	Maximum work time
w_{min}	Minimum paid work time
X_m	State of site m
$\bar{x}$	Optimal solution of the restricted master problem
x_{ijv}	Decision variable, if vehicle v travels from node i to node j
x_{ij}	Decision variable, if traveling from node i to node j
x_j	Decision variable, if duty j is chosen or not
γ_{iv}	Decision variable, if vehicle v includes node i
y_{ij}	Vehicle load from node i to node j
Z	Number of nodes in a path
z^*	Upper bound for the optimal solution of master problem
$\bar{z}$	Optimal solution of master problem
z	Index of node in a path

1 Introduction

1.1 Motivation

The service industry has grown considerably over the last decades and is expected to continue to grow. The average growth rate of services has been 2.9% per year between 1999 and 2009 (The World Bank (2011b)) and about 64% of the global gross national income is generated by services (The World Bank (2011a)). There exists a wide range of maintenance services that are offered, such as maintaining equipment in offices or factories, cleaning sites, replenishing retail outlets with products, or replenishing ATMs with bank notes. For some of these services, a service crew member must visit the site by a predetermined time. For instance, a copy machine must be serviced after a certain number of copies have been made, a site must be cleaned after a certain time interval, and an ATM must be replenished after certain amounts have been withdrawn.

We encountered such a problem at a major European service company. The company is maintaining restaurants, rest areas, etc., and guarantees that a site is serviced within pre-specified time intervals. In this application, the time of a service depends on the time of the previous maintenance at the site and the usage rate. The earliest service time is immediately after the current service; the latest service time is after a certain number of customers have visited the site.

One of the challenges that the company faces is efficient service crew planning. The service crew plan determines the times of the services and the routing of the service personnel simultaneously and we refer to this problem as the *service routing problem*. Historically, service times were taken as given and a service plan was developed that ensured that the services could be completed at minimal cost. One unused degree of freedom was the possibility to advance a service, i.e., to service a site before its latest

N. Holtvogt, *The Service Routing Problem*, Edition KWV,
https://doi.org/10.1007/978-3-658-24126-1_1

service time. Advancing a service can be beneficial, if the resulting service plan can be completed more efficiently than the original plan. However, if services are advanced, the total number of services increases and a trade-off decision must be made between advancing services and the increasing number of services.

Figures 1.1 and 1.2 illustrate this problem for an example with one depot, two sites, and three services at each site. Labor cost is 8.15 €/h and travel cost is 0.30 €/km.

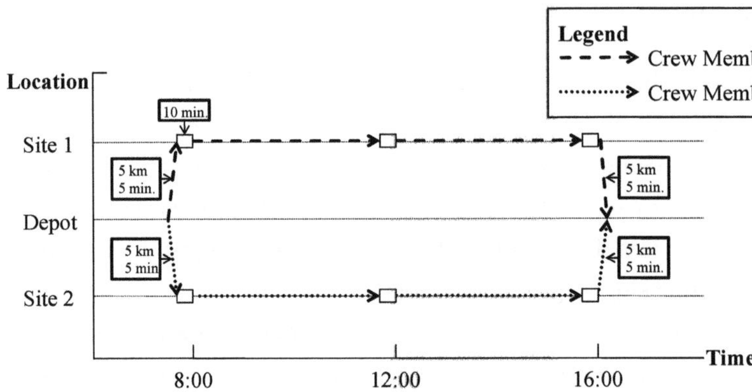

# Crew Member	2
Labor Cost	16 hours 40 minutes = 135.83 €
Travel Cost	20 km = 6 €
Total Cost	141.83 €

Figure 1.1: Example: Service at Latest Service Time

In Figure 1.1, services take place at the latest service times. The latest service times are the same for both sites (8:00, 12:00, and 16:00). It is required that service is terminated at the latest service times. With a service time of 10 minutes, the latest starting times are 7:50, 11:50, and 15:50. Two service crew members are required to fulfill all service requirements on time, resulting in total cost of 141.83 €.

In Figure 1.2, we have advanced all services of site 1 by 20 minutes assuming a travel time of 10 minutes from one site to the other site. Then, one service crew member can perform all services. The service crew member in the solution with service advance-

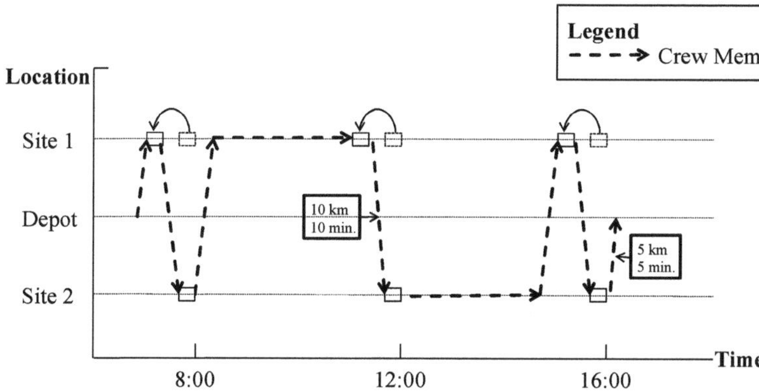

# Crew Member	1
Labor Cost	8 hours 40 minutes = 70.63 €
Travel Cost	60 km = 18 €
Total Cost	88.63 €

Figure 1.2: Example: Advanced Service

ment must travel more than in the solution without advancement. Consequently, the travel cost increases from 6 € to 18 €. But the labor cost decreases from 135.83 € to 70.63 €. In total, the service advancement leads to a cost decrease from 141.83 € to 88.63 €.

The objective of this thesis is to meet the challenges illustrated by the example and to develop solution approaches that optimize delivery times and crew scheduling cost jointly.

1.2 Structure of the Thesis

In this section, we describe the structure of the thesis. After the introduction, the thesis consists of seven main chapters and finalizes with a summary. Figure 1.3 illustrates the context of the chapters. First, Chapters 2 - 4 present the fundamental basics of this thesis. After the description of the service routing problem in Chapter 5, a framework to optimize the problem is developed (Chapters 6 and 7). Finally, the computational results are reported in Chapter 8.

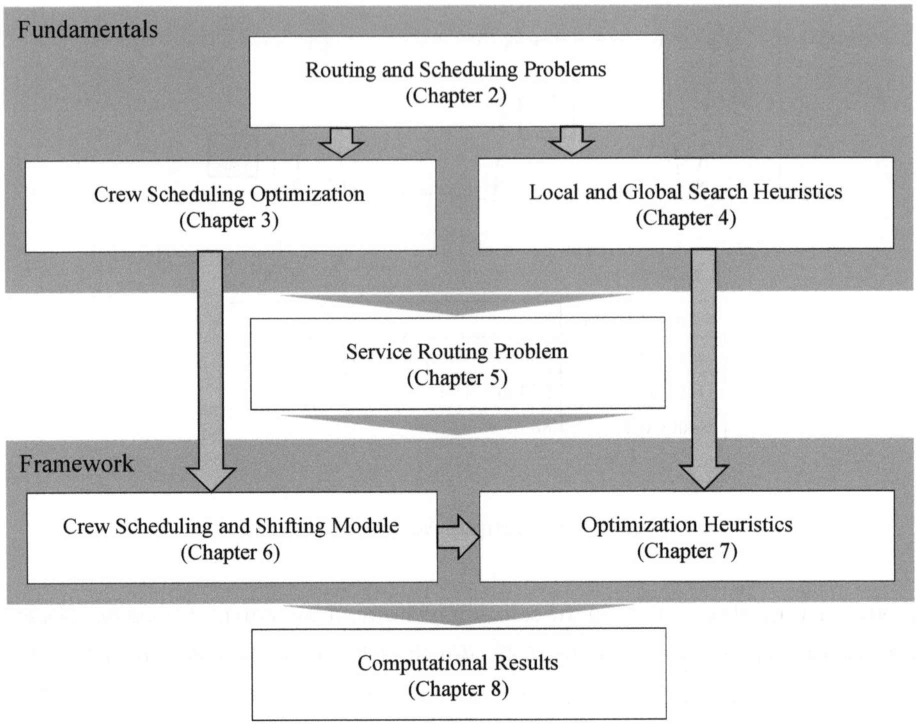

Figure 1.3: Structure of Thesis

The first part of this thesis (Chapters 2 - 4) provides the theoretical fundamentals for the service routing problem and the corresponding framework.

Chapter 2 reviews common routing and scheduling models to understand the basics and to identify possible solution approaches. The chapter starts with the description of routing problems. To give a comprehensive overview of the different models, the explanations follow the historical development of the problems. We start with the origin of routing problems: the traveling salesman problem. Then, we describe how this problem is linked to the classical vehicle routing problem and to the vehicle routing problem with time windows. Then, we demonstrate the crew scheduling problem whose solution approaches can possibly be applied to the service routing problem with fixed delivery times. The last problem described is the inventory routing problem that has some similarities to the service routing problem. The chapter concludes with a short summary of the main findings.

Chapter 3 provides a comprehensive overview of solution approaches for the crew scheduling problem. These solution approaches are of great interest for our service routing problem, because they may be used to solve the service routing problem for fixed service delivery times (Chapter 6).

Chapter 4 describes the fundamental basics of selected local and global search heuristics identified in Chapter 2. First, common local search heuristics are reviewed: local random search and steepest descent. Then, simulated annealing and tabu search are described as useful global search heuristics that may enable the solution to escape from local optima. In the course of this thesis, these approaches will be adapted to identify service delivery times to be shifted (Chapter 7).

After providing the theoretical fundamentals in Chapters 2 - 4, the subsequent chapters focus on the service routing problem and develop solution approaches to optimize it.

Chapter 5 gives a detailed description of the service routing problem, the subject of this thesis. The problem and its characteristics are explained in detail. Furthermore, specific terms are defined and linked to each other. The chapter also illustrates the importance to shift service delivery times.

Chapter 6 develops two modules: a crew scheduling module and a shifting module. Both are part of the optimization heuristics for the service routing problem designed in Chapter 7. The crew scheduling module determines optimal crew schedules for the service routing problem with fixed service delivery times. We adapt the branch-and-price approach described in Chapter 3 to develop an appropriate algorithm for the special requirements of the service routing problem. Then, a shifting module is designed to evaluate the option to shift a service, which is a key issue of the optimization heuristics in Chapter 7.

Chapter 7 combines both modules to develop optimization heuristics for the service routing problem. First, we design two approaches to find local optima for the service routing problem by applying the local search heuristics described in Chapter 4. Then, we extend the approaches by global search heuristics to possibly escape from local optima.

Chapter 8 applies the approaches developed in the previous chapters to different test scenarios and reports computational results. To analyze the potential of advancing services, we compare the cost of the solutions of the heuristics with the cost of a benchmark solution.

The thesis concludes with a summary followed by a critical review of the developed optimization heuristics. An outlook on possible extensions of the service routing problem and the heuristics is given.

1.3 Contribution of the Thesis

To our best knowledge, the service routing problem has not yet been dealt with in the literature. The characteristic of the problem is the combination of service crew scheduling and the shifting of service times. We model the problem and develop solution approaches. Besides designing new algorithms, we adapt and extend existing approaches.

Our developed solution approaches are based on two new modules: a crew scheduling module and a shifting module. The crew scheduling module quickly solves the crew scheduling problem with fixed delivery times to optimality by a modification of the prominent approach of Barnhart et al. (1998a) and Savelsbergh (2001). We model the network of the service routing problem in a graph. The graph is based on efficient arc and node construction procedures. To identify possible crew plans, we develop a depth-first search algorithm. Furthermore, we determine good upper bounds for the adapted branch-and-price approach to speed up the solution process. The development of powerful routines to identify feasible service duties leads to significant run time improvements and manageable memory requirements. The shifting module includes the new idea of local and best local shifts. The module provides an essential basis for our solution approaches.

Additionally, the developed optimization heuristics lead to high cost savings compared to a benchmark solution that does not take the shifting of services into account.

We provide further valuable insights for the service industries. We analyze, for instance, the effect of different work time regulations and demand characteristics.

Parts of this thesis appear in the working paper of Holtvogt and Thonemann (2011).

2 Routing and Scheduling Problems

The service routing problem belongs to the class of routing and scheduling problems. The literature provides multiple approaches to solve these problems. This chapter will give an overview of different models and the corresponding solution approaches to identify possible applicable approaches for the service routing problem. First, we introduce the traveling salesman problem in Section 2.1. Next, Section 2.2 describes the classical vehicle routing problem as an extension of the traveling salesman problem. By adding time windows, the vehicle routing problem results in the vehicle routing problem with time windows (Section 2.3). In Section 2.4, the crew scheduling problem is introduced. Then, the inventory routing problem is reviewed in Section 2.5. Finally, we summarize the main findings of the proposed routing and scheduling problems in Section 2.6.

2.1 Traveling Salesman Problem

2.1.1 Problem Description

The objective of the traveling salesman problem is the minimization of the total distance traveled by a salesman, who has to visit a predetermined number of cities before returning to the city where he started. Each city has to be visited exactly once by a single tour (Laporte (1992a)). Figure 2.1 illustrates the tour that a salesman can take to visit each city represented by a round-trip.

Among the first who considered the traveling salesman problem were Dantzig et al. (1954). They used several methods of combinatorial optimization and integer programming to solve a problem with 49 cities. The following explanations are in accordance to Laporte (1992a) and Domschke and Scholl (2010).

N. Holtvogt, *The Service Routing Problem*, Edition KWV,
https://doi.org/10.1007/978-3-658-24126-1_2

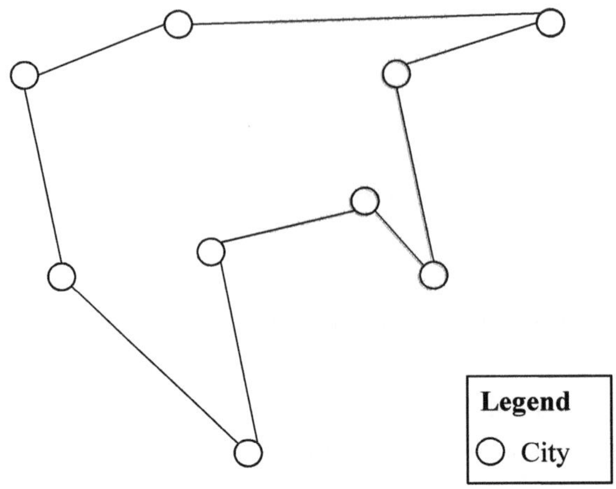

Figure 2.1: Traveling Salesman Problem

We base the formulation of the traveling salesman problem on a directed graph: Let G be a directed graph and all cities are represented by nodes $1, 2, \ldots, n$ of graph G. The set of all nodes is denoted by V. The set of all arcs is A and represents all connections between the cities. Each arc (i, j) $(i, j \in V)$ is associated with cost $c_{ij} \geq 0$. The variables x_{ij} denote the decision variables and are defined as follows:

$$x_{ij} = \begin{cases} 1, & \text{if the salesman drives directly from city } i \in V \text{ to city } j \in V \\ 0, & \text{else.} \end{cases}$$

Then, the traveling salesman problem is formulated as follows:

$$\min \quad \sum_{i \in V} \sum_{j \in V} c_{ij} x_{ij} \tag{2.1}$$

$$s.t. \quad \sum_{i \in V} x_{ij} = 1 \qquad \forall j \in V \tag{2.2}$$

$$\sum_{j \in V} x_{ij} = 1 \qquad \forall i \in V \tag{2.3}$$

$$x_{ij} \in \{0, 1\} \qquad \forall i, j \in V \tag{2.4}$$

$$Subtour \quad Elimination \quad Constraints. \tag{2.5}$$

The objective of the traveling salesman problem is to minimize the total cost (2.1). Equations (2.2) and (2.3) ensure that each city is visited exactly once. That means that each node is entered (Equations (2.2)) and left exactly once (Equations (2.3)). Constraints (2.4) guarantee that x_{ij} are binary decision variables.

The traveling salesman has to visit all cities by a single tour. Therefore, subtours are undesirable. A subtour is a tour on a subset of less than n cities. To avoid subtours, subtour elimination constraints (Constraints (2.5)) have to be added to Equations (2.1)-(2.4). The most common subtour elimination constraints are the Dantzig-Fulkerson-Johnson (Dantzig et al. (1954)) or the Miller-Tucker-Zemlin (Miller et al. (1960)) subtour elimination constraints.

Dantzig-Fulkerson-Johnson Subtour Elimination Constraints Let S be a subset of set V. Then, the following constraints prohibit the formation of subtours:

$$\sum_{i\in V}\sum_{j\in V} x_{ij} \leq |S|-1, S\subset V, 2\leq |S| \leq n-2. \tag{2.6}$$

In case of a subtour of subset S, the corresponding subtour would contain $|S|$ nodes. Then, Constraints (2.6) were violated, since $\sum_{i\in V}\sum_{j\in V} x_{ij}$ would be equal to $|S|$, which is greater than $|S|-1$. Since a subtour over one node cannot occur, it suffices to define Constraints (2.6) for $2\leq |S| \leq n-2$.

Miller-Tucker-Zemlin Subtour Elimination Constraints For the Miller-Tucker-Zemlin subtour elimination constraints, an arbitrary real number u_i is introduced for each node $i\in V\setminus\{1\}$. Then, the subtour elimination constraints are as follows:

$$u_i - u_j + (n-1)x_{ij} \leq n-2, \qquad \forall i \in V\setminus\{1\}, i\neq j \tag{2.7}$$

$$1\leq u_i \leq n-1, \qquad \forall i \in V\setminus\{1\}. \tag{2.8}$$

Constraints (2.7) prohibit tours with fewer than n nodes and Constraints (2.8) ensure that variables u_i are unique for any feasible tour. Compared to Constraints (2.6), Constraints (2.7) and (2.8) reduce the number of constraints.

Although the Miller-Tucker-Zemlin formulation is more compact than the Dantzig-Fulkerson-Johnson formulation, its linear relaxation is generally weaker than the one of the Dantzig-Fulkerson-Johnson formulation.

2.1.2 Solution Approaches

The traveling salesman problem is NP-hard (Lenstra and Kan (1981)). However, multiple heuristic and exact algorithms have been developed to solve the traveling salesman problem.

2.1.2.1 Heuristic Algorithms

Most heuristic approaches are based on two procedures. In a first step, an initial tour is generated by a tour construction procedure. In a second step, the tour is improved by a tour improvement procedure. In this section, we will focus on the most commonly used tour construction and tour improvement procedures according to Laporte (1992a).

Tour Construction Tour construction heuristics expand already existing routes by inserting uncovered customers to generate new tours or to expand existing ones.

> *Nearest Neighbor*
> The algorithm starts with a randomly chosen node $n_1 \in V$ (Bellmore and Nemhauser (1968)). In each iteration, the tour is expanded by the node that is not part of the tour and that has the lowest distance to the last node considered. After adding the last node to the tour, the corresponding node is linked to the first node n_1 of the tour. The best tour is found by considering all nodes as possible starting points.
>
> *Insertion Heuristics*
> Insertion heuristics expand successively a tour until a feasible round-trip is obtained. The algorithm starts with a tour consisting of two nodes. Based on a certain criterion, a node is chosen that is inserted in the tour. The algorithm was first introduced by Karg and Thompson (1964).

Patching Algorithm

The approach was developed by Karp (1979) for directed graphs. The idea is to solve the traveling salesman problem (2.1)-(2.4) with a cost matrix ignoring any subtour elimination constraints. If the solution contains subtours, the subtours are connected one after another. In each iteration, the increase of the objective function value is minimized.

Tour Improvement Tour improvement heuristics are approaches to improve existing routes. Initial routes are often generated by tour construction heuristics.

RO-opt Algorithm

The RO-opt algorithm was introduced by Lin (1965) with the detailed description of 3-opt tours. The approach starts with an initial tour and has the objective to find the shortest tour. Then, *RO* arcs are removed from the tour and the nodes are reconnected. If a shorter tour occurs, the tour becomes the new tour. If no improvements can be found, the algorithm terminates. The resulting tour is referred to as RO-opt tour. The RO-opt algorithm has been improved by different methods. For instance, Lin and Kernighan (1973) introduced an approach with dynamically modified values of *RO*. Extensions to the approach have been provided by Frieze et al. (1982), Kanellakis and Papadimitriou (1980), and Nurmi (1991).

Simulated Annealing

Simulated annealing is based on a connection between the multivariate or combinatorial optimization and the material annealing process used in statistical mechanics, i.e., a discipline of condensed matter physics (Metropolis et al. (1953), Kirkpatrick et al. (1983)). Kirkpatrick et al. (1983) illustrate the determination of the low-temperature state of a material. The objective is to reduce the defects caused by non-optimal cooling. The material is heated until its particles are randomly distributed in the liquid state, i.e., the particles escape from their initial positions (local optima). Then, the temperature is lowered slowly. The particles move randomly from one state to another state and may find a better configuration with lower internal energy than in the initial positions. The slow decrease of the temperature avoids, for instance, that the resulting crystal will have defects. This procedure provides a framework to solve large problem instances and to reduce the risk of getting stuck in a local optimum.

Since we will apply simulated annealing to identify good delivery points for the service routing problem, the approach will be described in detail in Section 4.2.1. Examples for the application of simulated annealing to the traveling salesman problem are given by Bonomi and Lutton (1984), Kirkpatrick (1984), Golden and Skiscim (1986), and Nahar et al. (1986).

Tabu Search
The idea of tabu search is based on the examination of neighbors of a solution, i.e., solutions that are closely related to the current solution. The approach also tries to avoid a local minimum. Additionally, cyclic solutions are avoided by forbidding the examination of already analyzed solutions for several iterations by putting the corresponding solutions on a tabu list (Glover (1986)).

Like simulated annealing, tabu search will be applied to our service routing problem. Consequently, more details on the approach are provided in Section 4.2.2. Examples for the application of tabu search to the traveling salesman problem are given by Malek et al. (1989), Fiechter (1994), or Knox (1994).

2.1.2.2 Exact Algorithms

The most common exact algorithms to solve the traveling salesman problem rely on branch-and-bound approaches (Domschke and Scholl (2010)). The general approach of branch-and-bound is the repeated partitioning (branching) of the space of all feasible solutions into smaller subsets. A lower bound for the cost of the solutions within each subset is determined. Subsets with a bound greater than the cost of a known feasible solution are excluded from further partitionings. The partitioning continues until a feasible solution is found with cost not greater than the bound for any subset (Lawler and Wood (1966)).

A good lower bound of the optimal solution provides the base for a good solution approach. It helps to exclude unprofitable subsets as early as possible. In the following, different approaches to obtain a lower bound are described.

AP-Relaxation If we relax the subtour elimination constraints (2.5) and relax Constraints (2.4) to $x_{ij} \geq 0$, we obtain an assignment problem (AP) with Equations (2.1) - (2.3). The solution of the AP represents an initial lower bound for the optimal solution to the traveling salesman problem (Laporte (1992a)). There are multiple approaches based on AP-relaxation, e.g., Little et al. (1963), Bellmore and Malone (1971), Garfinkel (1973), or Carpaneto et al. (1995). We will focus on the most common approaches of Carpaneto and Toth (1980), Balas and Christofides (1981), and Miller and Pekny (1991).

Carpaneto and Toth (1980)
Carpaneto and Toth (1980) apply a modified AP. At a generic node of the search tree, some decision variables x_{ij} are set equal to 0 or 1. If the solution has no subtours, the solution is feasible. Otherwise, one of the subtours is selected. Then, subproblems are created in which all arcs of the selected subtour are executed. The branching is performed using a breadth-first rule, i.e., branching is always performed at the node with the lowest cost of the modified AP.

Balas and Christofides (1981)
Balas and Christofides (1981) use a Lagrangian problem to determine a lower bound of the traveling salesman problem. At every node of the search tree, the lower bound is determined based on the Lagrangian multiplier and the dual variables of the AP.

Miller and Pekny (1991)
The algorithm of Miller and Pekny (1991) determines disjoint sets that are based on an optimal solution to the AP. They splice two or more cycles in an AP solution into a possibly suboptimal Hamiltonian cycle. The idea is to reduce the solution of the traveling salesman problem to the solution of a Hamiltonian cycle problem on a suitable graph. This so-called Hamiltonian cycle problem

reduction is added to the basic branch-and-bound approach to quickly find a solution of the traveling salesman problem.

Fischetti and Toth (1997) show that the AP-based approaches are not satisfying for some cases. To solve difficult problem instances, a branch-and-cut algorithm is developed. The approach is a lowest-first branch-and-bound procedure. They compute a lower bound by a linear program relaxation (LP-relaxation) that is expanded by so-called facet-defining cuts. Separation algorithms identify facet-defining traveling salesman problem inequalities that cut off the current linear program (LP) optimal solution.

r-Arborescense F Fischetti and Toth (1992) base their approach on spanning arborescences. They apply a shortest spanning r-arborescence problem (r-SAP) to determine a lower bound to the optimal solution of the traveling salesman problem. The r-SAP is decomposed into two subproblems. There are multiple extensions of the r-arborescence-relaxation. The interested reader is referred to Held and Karp (1970) or Domschke and Scholl (2010) for possible approaches.

2.1.3 Conclusion

For the traveling salesman problem, we presented heuristic and exact solution approaches. For large problem instances, exact solution approaches do not often lead to the optimal solution within acceptable computational time. Therefore, heuristic solution approaches are preferred. Generally, most methods are based on tour construction and/or improvement procedures. Generalized insertion and tabu search approaches are known to be the most powerful methods (Laporte (1992a)).

2.2 Vehicle Routing Problem

2.2.1 Problem Description

The vehicle routing problem is an extension of the traveling salesman problem, where multiple vehicles located at a central depot have to visit a set of customers.

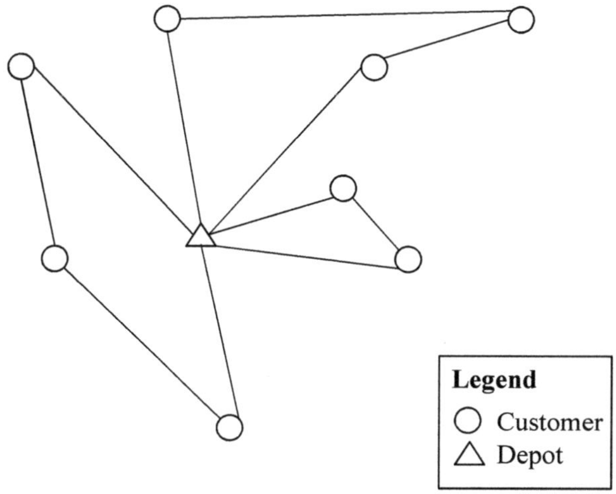

Figure 2.2: Vehicle Routing Problem

Figure 2.2 illustrates the vehicle routing problem (Giaglis et al. (2004)). The triangle represents the single depot. Each vehicle has to start and end its tour at the depot. Because of capacity constraints for the vehicles, multiple tours may be necessary to visit all customers. The typical objective of the vehicle routing problem is to minimize the overall distribution cost by constructing feasible tours with respect to given constraints. The classical vehicle routing problem with a single depot is defined as follows (Laporte (2009)):

Let VE be a homogeneous fleet of vehicles, $N = 1, \ldots, n$ a set of customers with demand d_i $(i \in N)$ and G a directed graph. All customers are represented by nodes $1, 2, \ldots, n$ of graph G. The depot is divided into node 0 for the starting depot and node $n+1$ for the ending depot. The set of all nodes is denoted by V. The set of all arcs A represents all connections among the customers and between the customers and the depot. No arc starts at node $n+1$ and no arc ends in node 0. Each arc $(i, j) \in V$ is associated with cost $c_{ij} \geq 0$. The capacity of a vehicle $v \in VE$ is denoted by Q and the decision variables x_{ijv} are defined by:

$$x_{ijv} = \begin{cases} 1, & \text{if vehicle } v \in VE \text{ drives directly from node } i \in V \text{ to node } j \in V \\ 0, & \text{else.} \end{cases}$$

The vehicle routing problem can be formulated as follows:

$$\min \quad \sum_{v \in VE} \sum_{i \in V} \sum_{j \in V} c_{ij} x_{ijv} \tag{2.9}$$

$$s.t. \quad \sum_{v \in VE} \sum_{j \in V} x_{ijv} = 1 \qquad \forall i \in N \tag{2.10}$$

$$\sum_{i \in V} d_i \sum_{j \in V} x_{ijv} \leq Q \qquad \forall v \in VE \tag{2.11}$$

$$\sum_{j \in V \setminus \{0\}} x_{0jv} = 1 \qquad \forall v \in VE \tag{2.12}$$

$$\sum_{i \in V \setminus \{n+1\}} x_{ihv} - \sum_{j \in V \setminus \{0\}} x_{hjv} = 0 \qquad \forall v \in VE, h \in N \tag{2.13}$$

$$\sum_{i \in V \setminus \{n+1\}} x_{i(n+1)v} = 1 \qquad \forall v \in VE \tag{2.14}$$

$$x_{ijv} \in \{0,1\} \qquad \forall v \in VE, i, j \in V. \tag{2.15}$$

The objective of the vehicle routing problem is to minimize the total cost (Equation (2.9)). Equations (2.10) guarantee that each customer is visited exactly once. Equations (2.11) limit the total capacity of each vehicle. Equations (2.12)-(2.14) ensure the flow conservation: each vehicle has to leave the depot (Equations (2.12)) and has to arrive at the depot (Equations (2.14)). Additionally, the number of arriving vehicles at all nodes has to equal the number of departing vehicles (Equations (2.13)). Constraints (2.15) impose binary conditions on the variables.

2.2.2 Solution Approaches

The vehicle routing problem is a combinatorial optimization problem and is - like the traveling salesman problem - NP-hard (Prins (2004)). Various approaches for solving the vehicle routing problem have been developed during the last decades. These can be divided into heuristic and exact approaches.

2.2.2.1 Heuristic Algorithms

Some of the heuristic approaches of the traveling salesman problem described in Section 2.1 can be applied to the vehicle routing problem (Laporte (1992b)). The nearest neighbor heuristics (Tyagi (1968), Van Breedam (2002)), insertion heuristics (Mole and Jameson (1976)), and improving heuristics (Russell (1977)) can easily be adapted to the vehicle routing problem without major modifications. Other possible heuristic approaches have been developed including saving algorithms, set partitioning heuristics, cluster-first/route-second heuristics, and heuristics such as local search, genetic algorithms and ant colony optimization heuristics ((Laporte (1992b)), Laporte (2009)). In the following, we will focus on these approaches.

Saving Algorithms The saving algorithm was developed by Clarke and Wright (1964). The algorithm starts with the construction of routes for each customer. Initially, each route starts at the depot denoted by 0, followed by the visit of a customer $i \in N$ and then the route ends at the depot. In each iteration, routes are merged, such that the maximum savings are reached, i.e., a route ending with customer i is merged with the route starting at customer j with $j = \arg\max\{c_{i0} + c_{0k} - c_{ik} | k \in N\}$. If no merges are possible, the algorithm terminates. Multiple extensions of the algorithm have been developed to reduce the complexity of the approach (Golden et al. (1977), Paessens (1988), and Wark and Holt (1994)).

Set Partitioning Heuristics The most commonly used approach is the sweep algorithm of Gillett and Miller (1974). The general idea of the approach is the representation of nodes by their polar coordinates. One starts with the assignment of an angle value $\Theta_i = 0$ to a randomly chosen node $i \in N$. Then, all other coordinates are determined relative to Θ_i and the nodes are ordered with increasing value of their corresponding angles. The process starts with the unrouted node $i \in N$ with the smallest Θ_i. The node is assigned to a predetermined vehicle. More nodes are assigned to the vehicle until the capacity constraints are met. If all nodes have been assigned to a vehicle, a traveling salesman problem is solved for each vehicle. If applicable, nodes are exchanged between routes to improve the overall cost. For other set partitioning approaches, the interested reader is referred to Foster and Ryan (1981) and Renaud et al. (1996).

Cluster-First/Route-Second Heuristics Cluster-first/route-second heuristics have been provided by Fisher and Jaikumar (1981). The approach is performed in two steps based on sweep and saving algorithms. First, a generalized assignment problem is solved to identify clusters. Then, a route is built for each cluster by solving a traveling salesman problem. The approach to identify clusters has been studied by Baker and Sheasby (1999).

Local Search Heuristics Local search heuristics move from one solution to another within a neighborhood (Voudouris (1999)). The objective is to explore the solution space in an efficient way. As we want to base the shifting of service deliveries on local search in this thesis, the approach is described in detail in Section 4.1.

Examples for local search heuristics include variable neighborhood searches (Kytöjoki et al. (2007)), very large neighborhood searches (Ergun et al. (2006)), and adaptive large neighborhood searches (Pisinger and Ropke (2007)).

Genetic Algorithms Genetic algorithms have been introduced by Holland (1975). The algorithms start with any initial solution. Then, a parent solution is selected from the current solution. Offspring solutions are generated and poor solutions are replaced to generate a new population (Mitchell (1998)). For the solution of the vehicle routing problem, genetic algorithms are often combined with local search. Examples have been provided most recently by Prins (2009) and Nagata and Bräysy (2009).

Ant Colony Optimization Heuristics Ant colony optimization heuristics belong to the methods of learning mechanism heuristics. The approach has its origin in the actions of real ants hunting for food (Bell and Mcmullen (2004)). A single ant is not effective in its actions, but an ant colony is able to solve complex problems. The communication between ants is based on pheromones that ants lay on their paths, so that other ants will follow. The more ants follow a path, the more attractive is the corresponding path due to the pheromones of all ants passing this path. The optimization approach adapts this idea by increasing the weight of an arc that is used in multiple good solutions. Bell and Mcmullen (2004), Reimann (2004), and Yu et al. (2009) provide ant colony optimization heuristics to solve the vehicle routing problem.

2.2.2.2 Exact Algorithms

The most common exact approaches are branch-and-bound algorithms, linear programming problems such as vehicle flow, commodity flow and set partitioning problems including column generation, and dynamic programming (Laporte (2009)). The approaches will be described in this section.

Branch-and-Bound Algorithms In the last decades, multiple branch-and-bound algorithms for solving the vehicle routing problem have been developed, e.g., by Christofides et al. (1981) and Fisher (1994). As for the traveling salesman problem, the general idea is to determine a feasible solution by an enumerative process. However, most approaches for the vehicle routing problem do not rely on the relaxation of the underlying problem, but on the computation of a shortest spanning tree bound at each node. A good lower bound is of importance for the efficiency of branch-and-bound approaches. For instance, Christofides et al. (1981) present an approach that incorporates lower bounds computed from shortest spanning κ-degree center tree and q-routes. Improved branch-and-bound approaches have been proposed by Fisher (1994).

Vehicle Flow Problems The vehicle routing problem can be formulated as a vehicle flow problem based on the formulation of the traveling salesman problem with Dantzig-Fulkerson-Johnson subtour elimination constraints (2.1)-(2.6) (Laporte and Nobert (1983)). The vehicle flow problem focuses on the number of vehicles needed to serve all customers. It is formulated as follows (Toth and Vigo (2002)):

$$\min \quad \sum_{i \in V} \sum_{j \in V} c_{ij} x_{ij} \tag{2.16}$$

$$s.t. \quad \sum_{i \in V} x_{ij} = 1 \qquad \forall j \in N \tag{2.17}$$

$$\sum_{j \in V} x_{ij} = 1 \qquad \forall i \in N \tag{2.18}$$

$$\sum_{j \in V \setminus \{0\}} x_{0j} = VE \tag{2.19}$$

$$\sum_{i \in V \setminus \{n+1\}} x_{i(n+1)} = VE \tag{2.20}$$

$$\sum_{i \in S} \sum_{j \in S} x_{ij} \leq |S| - v(S) \qquad \forall S \subseteq N, S \neq \emptyset \tag{2.21}$$

$$x_{ij} \in \{0,1\} \qquad \forall i,j \in V. \tag{2.22}$$

The objective is to minimize the total cost (2.16). Equations (2.17) and (2.18) guarantee that one arc enters each node and leaves each node. Equations (2.19) and (2.20) ensure the flow conservation. Equations (2.21) ensure that at least $v(S)$ arcs leave each customer set S. To take care of capacity constraints, it holds that $v(S) = \frac{\sum_{i \in S} d_i}{Q}$, i.e., the minimum number of vehicles needed to serve S is equal to the sum of the demands divided by the capacity of each vehicle. Constraints (2.22) ensure binary decision variables.

To solve the vehicle routing problem as a vehicle flow problem, most approaches are based on branch-and-bound algorithms (Desrochers et al. (1985)). Laporte (2009) provide a more detailed description of the solution approaches.

The vehicle flow models are often used for the basic vehicle routing problem. The models are mostly not suitable for practical issues, for instance, if the cost of the solution depends on the overall sequence of nodes.

Commodity Flow Problems The vehicle routing problem can also be formulated as a commodity flow model. The model focuses on the vehicle loads flowing through the network. For the vehicle routing problem, the formulation is as follows (Toth and Vigo (2002) and Baldacci et al. (2004)):

$$\min \quad \sum_{i \in V} \sum_{j \in V} c_{ij} x_{ij} \tag{2.23}$$

$$s.t. \quad \sum_{j \in V} (y_{ji} - y_{ij}) = 2d_i \qquad \forall i \in N \tag{2.24}$$

$$\sum_{j \in N} y_{0j} = \sum_{i \in N} d_i \tag{2.25}$$

$$\sum_{j \in N} y_{j0} = (VE)Q - \sum_{i \in N} d_i \tag{2.26}$$

$$\sum_{j \in N} y_{(n+1)j} = (VE)Q \tag{2.27}$$

$$y_{ij} + y_{ji} = Q x_{ij} \qquad \forall (i,j) \in A \tag{2.28}$$

$$\sum_{i<j,\, j \in V} x_{ij} - \sum_{i>j,\, j \in V} x_{ji} = 2 \qquad \forall i \in N \tag{2.29}$$

$$y_{ij}, y_{ji} \geq 0 \qquad \forall (i,j) \in A \tag{2.30}$$

$$x_{ij} \in \{0,1\} \qquad \forall i,j \in V. \tag{2.31}$$

y_{ij} denotes the vehicle load from node i to node j and $y_{ji} = Q - y_{ij}$ represents the vehicle residual capacity, if a vehicle drives from i to j, i.e., $x_{ij} = 1$. VE denotes again the number of vehicles of the homogeneous fleet and d_i denotes the demand rate of customer i. Equations (2.24) - (2.27) guarantee the flow conservation. Equations (2.28) ensure the feasibility of variables y_{ij} and y_{ji}. Equations (2.29) assure that any feasible solution contains two arcs for each customer. The commodity flow model can be solved, for instance, by a branch-and-cut algorithm (Baldacci et al. (2004)).

Commodity flow models are often used as a basis for the exact solution to the vehicle routing problem. But the number of binary variables can become too large.

Set Partitioning Problems Besides the vehicle flow and commodity flow formulation, the vehicle routing problem can also be formulated as a set partitioning problem. The formulation of a problem as a set partitioning problem will be described in detail in Section 3.2.1, as it is part of our solution approach for the service routing problem with fixed delivery times. The most common approach to solve a vehicle routing problem by a partitioning problem is column generation ((Desrosiers et al.

(1984), Agarwal et al. (1989), Desrochers et al. (1990))). Multiple approaches have been developed for instance by Lysgaard et al. (2004), Fukasawa et al. (2005), or Baldacci et al. (2007).

Set partitioning models are often applied for very general route cost. In contrast to vehicle flow and commodity flow formulations, the linear programming relaxation of the set partitioning formulation is much tighter.

Dynamic Programming The general approach of dynamic programming is the division of the problem into multiple subproblems. The optimal solutions of the smaller problem instances should provide the optimal solution of the larger problem instances (Dreyfus and Law (1977)). By evaluating different states of the system, the optimization problem can be transformed into the recursive solution of a sequence of subproblems (Cervellera et al. (2006)).

The vehicle routing problem was first formulated as a dynamic program by Eilon et al. (1971). For the detailed model formulation, we refer to Laporte (2009). An efficient dynamic program approach requires a reduction of the state space by dominance, feasibility criteria, or relaxation procedures. Christofides et al. (1981) provides a state space relaxation algorithm to reduce the state space.

2.2.3 Conclusion

For the vehicle routing problem, we described heuristic and exact solution approaches. The problem has a higher complexity than the traveling salesman problem. Additionally, exact methods are not very flexible. Therefore, heuristic approaches are often preferred to quickly determine good solutions for large-scale problems. Heuristics like local search are widely applied due to their simplicity and flexibility to handle multiple different constraints (Laporte (2009)).

2.3 Vehicle Routing Problem with Time Windows

2.3.1 Problem Description

An extension of the vehicle routing problem is the vehicle routing problem with time windows (Cordeau et al. (2002)). The characteristic is that each vehicle must arrive at a customer at a pre-specified time. The vehicle routing problem with time windows is also defined on a graph $G = (V, A)$ with start depot node 0 and end depot node $n+1$. $N = 1, ..., n$ denotes again the set of nodes representing the customers. Each customer $i \in N$ is associated with a time window $\left[b_i{}^{start}, b_i{}^{end}\right]$, i.e., a vehicle has to arrive at a customer i before b_i^{end}. The visit at a customer i is not possible before b_i^{start}, but the arrival can be before $b_i{}^{start}$.

For the start and end depot node it holds, that $[b_0{}^{start}, b_0{}^{end}] = [b_{n+1}^{start}, b_{n+1}{}^{end}] = [E, \Gamma]$. E denotes the earliest possible departure time from the depot and Γ the latest possible arrival time. Besides the cost c_{ij}, the arcs of the directed graph G are also associated with travel time including service time at node i, $t_{ij} \geq 0$. The starting time of a vehicle v at customer i is defined for each node i by the decision variable σ_{iv}. Each customer is associated with a certain demand d_i. At the depot no demand occurs, i.e., $d_0 = d_{n+1} = 0$. The decision variable x_{ijv} indicates if vehicle v drives from node i to j ($x_{ijv} = 1$) or not ($x_{ijv} = 0$). The formulation of the vehicle routing problem with time windows is as follows (Cordeau et al. (2002)):

$$\min \quad \sum_{v \in VE} \sum_{i \in V} \sum_{j \in V} c_{ij} x_{ijv} \tag{2.32}$$

$$s.t. \quad \sum_{v \in VE} \sum_{j \in V} x_{ijv} = 1 \qquad \forall i \in N \tag{2.33}$$

$$\sum_{i \in V} d_i \sum_{j \in V} x_{ijv} \leq Q \qquad \forall v \in VE \tag{2.34}$$

$$\sum_{j \in V \setminus \{0\}} x_{0jv} = 1 \qquad \forall v \in VE \tag{2.35}$$

$$\sum_{i \in V \setminus \{n+1\}} x_{ihv} - \sum_{j \in V \setminus \{0\}} x_{hjv} = 0 \qquad \forall v \in VE, h \in N \tag{2.36}$$

$$\sum_{i \in V \setminus \{n+1\}} x_{i(n+1)v} = 1 \qquad \forall v \in VE \tag{2.37}$$

$$x_{ijv}(\sigma_{iv} + t_{ij} - \sigma_{jv}) \leq 0 \qquad \forall v \in VE, i, j \in V \qquad (2.38)$$

$$b_i^{start}(\sum_{j \in V \setminus \{0\}} x_{ijv}) \leq \sigma_{iv} \leq b_i^{end}(\sum_{j \in V \setminus \{0\}} x_{ijv}) \qquad \forall v \in VE, i \in N \qquad (2.39)$$

$$E \leq \sigma_{iv} \leq \Gamma \qquad \forall v \in VE, i \in V \qquad (2.40)$$

$$x_{ijv} \in \{0,1\} \qquad \forall v \in VE, i, j \in V. \qquad (2.41)$$

Equations (2.32) - (2.37) and (2.41) are similar to Equations (2.9) - (2.15) of the vehicle routing problem. Equations (2.38) - (2.40) consider the time window constraints. Equations (2.38) ensure that no vehicle v can arrive at j before $\sigma_{iv} + t_{ij}$ if traveling from i to j. Constraints (2.39) state that the time window constraints are respected and leads to $\sigma_{iv} = 0$, if node i is not visited by vehicle v. Equations (2.40) consider the opening hours of the depot.

2.3.2 Solution Approaches

The vehicle routing problem with time windows is NP-hard (Desrosiers et al. (1995)). To solve the problem, multiple solution approaches have been developed. First, we provide an overview of several heuristic approaches. Then, we present exact solution approaches to derive an optimal non-integer solution. And finally, we show how optimal integer solutions can be obtained. We will see that some of the existing approaches for the vehicle routing problem can be enhanced to find solutions for the vehicle routing problem with time windows.

2.3.2.1 Heuristic Algorithms

Heuristic solution approaches were provided, e.g., by Koskosidis et al. (1992), Taillard et al. (1997), Potvin et al. (1996), and Potvin and Bengio (1996). We follow the description of Bräysy and Gendreau (2005a,b) to give a short overview of different heuristic approaches. First, we describe tour construction and tour improvement heuristics. Then, we review metaheuristics such as tabu search and evolutionary metaheuristics. Finally, we report other metaheuristics to solve the vehicle routing problem with time windows.

Tour Construction Similar to the tour construction heuristics described for the traveling salesman problem, the general idea is the extension of existing routes by inserting uncovered nodes. To guarantee feasibility of the routes, capacity and time window constraints have to be considered. Bräysy and Gendreau (2005a) discuss six different tour construction heuristics:

Route-First/Cluster-Second Heuristics
In contrast to the cluster-first/route-second heuristic described for the vehicle routing problem, route-first/cluster-second heuristics generate subtours after the determination of a tour. Based on a so-called giant tour that covers all nodes, clusters are built to determine smaller feasible tours (Solomon (1986)).

Saving Heuristics
Similar to the vehicle routing problem, saving heuristics for the vehicle routing problem with time windows are based on the algorithm developed by Clarke and Wright (1964). For the vehicle routing problem with time windows, additional constraints have to be considered by merging two routes. Further details on appropriate approaches are provided by Solomon (1987).

Time-Oriented Nearest Neighbor
For the time-oriented nearest neighbor approach, an initial tour is constructed for the customer with the lowest distance to the depot. Then, among all customers that are not part of any tour, the one with the closest distance to the last added customer is chosen and inserted into the tour. If the insertion of a new customer violates any constraint, a new tour is constructed. The construction of tours finishes with the insertion of the last customer (Solomon (1987)).

Time-Oriented Sweep Heuristic
The time-oriented sweep heuristic was developed by Solomon (1987) and is an extension of the sweep algorithm introduced by Gillett and Miller (1974)

described for the set partitioning heuristics to solve the vehicle routing problem. The general idea is to decompose the vehicle routing problem with time windows into a clustering and a scheduling problem. The clustering problem assigns customers to tours. Then, the scheduling problem schedules the customers based on the insertion heuristic described in the following.

Sequential Insertion Heuristics

For sequential insertion heuristics, an initial so-called partial tour is generated with a first customer. Then, customers are inserted until the constraints of the underlying problem are met. The process is repeated until no more customers are left. The choice of the first customer is described in detail by Solomon (1986). For the sequential insertion of customers to existing tours, Solomon (1987) proposes three different approaches:

The first approach aims to maximize the benefit to visit a customer by the considered partial tour compared to a direct tour. The second approach minimizes the total tour distance and time by inserting a customer that is not part of any tour. The third approach considers also the urgency of covering a customer. The first approach was proven to be the most successful in the study of Solomon (1987).

Parallel Insertion Heuristic

In contrast to sequential insertion heuristics, a parallel insertion heuristic constructs multiple tours simultaneously. Potvin and Rousseau (1993) developed an algorithm that generates tours in parallel. Using a generalized regret measure the next customer to be inserted is determined. The regret measure is based on Tillman and Cain (1972). The idea of Potvin and Rousseau (1993) is to quantify the absolute difference between the best and all other alternatives. Based on the regret value customers are chosen according to different considerations.

Tour Improvement Starting with an initial solution, tour improvement heuristics modify current tours to improve the solution quality (Cordeau et al. (2002)). In the following, we will describe the most common approaches according to the work of Bräysy and Gendreau (2005a).

Local Search Heuristics

Local search heuristics iteratively improve tours by examining the neighboring solutions. Depending on the approach, the first or the best found solution that satisfies a predetermined criterion is selected. More details on local search heuristics will be provided in Section 4.1.

i-Optimal Improvement Heuristics

The i-optimal search heuristics start with an i-exchange. An i-exchange describes the replacement of a set of i nodes by another set of i nodes in a tour. If the tour cannot be improved by an i-exchange, it is said to be i-optimal. i-optimal improvement heuristics have been developed for instance by Russell (1977) and Savelsbergh (1992).

Bi-Criteria Heuristics

Based on the saving algorithm by Clarke and Wright (1964) for the vehicle routing problem, Van Landeghem (1988) developed a bi-criteria heuristic. The heuristic is based on the saving algorithm and a time criterion. The time criterion measures the quality of a link between customers in terms of time.

2-opt Exchange Heuristic*

The 2-opt* exchange approach has been developed by Potvin and Rousseau (1995) and combines two tours by inserting the last customers of one tour (often the one with late time windows) after the first customers of another tour (often the one with early time windows). Potvin and Rousseau (1995) show that in particular a hybrid approach based on the 2-opt* and another node exchange heuristic is powerful.

Cyclic Transfer Algorithms

The cyclic transfer algorithms introduced by Thompson and Psaraftis (1993) exploit on the one hand the assignment of demands to vehicles and on the other hand the routing of vehicles through assigned demand stops. The basic idea of cyclic transfers is to minimize the cost of a set of tours by transferring demands among tours in a cyclical manner. The work of Thompson and Orlin (1989) provides a more detailed description of the theory of cyclic transfers.

Parallel Tour Construction Heuristics
The parallel tour construction approach of Antes and Derigs (1995) applies the concept of negotiation between customers and tours. The procedure leads to an algorithm with simultaneous construction and improvement of tours.

Alternate i-Exchange Reduction Approach
The alternate i-exchange reduction approach developed by Cordone and Calvo (2001) consists of the following procedures: First, the solution is improved by the i-opt exchange algorithm (see description above). Second, the number of vehicles is reduced by an ad-hoc approach. Third, a second objective function is applied to escape from a local optimum.

Three-Phase Approach
Bräysy (2002) introduced a deterministic local search approach based on three phases. The approach starts with the determination of an initial solution by a tour construction heuristic. In the second phase, the number of tours is reduced by a local search operator based on so-called ejection chains. Then, the local distance traveled is minimized by the Or-opt exchanges introduced by Or (1976).

Metaheuristics Metaheuristics are robust solution methods that help to escape from local optima and that are suitable for different problem types (Glover and Kochenberger (2003)). In the following, we present several metaheuristics including tabu search and evolutionary metaheuristics to solve the vehicle routing problem with time windows according to the work of Bräysy and Gendreau (2005b).

Tabu Search
Tabu search is described in detail in Section 4.2.2. Generally, the approach explores multiple neighborhood solutions and tries to avoid cyclic solutions by putting recently explored solutions on a tabu list (Glover (1986)). Tabu search

also accepts solutions that are worse than the current solution. Therefore, the search space is larger than the one of standard local search approaches. In the following, we report the most common metaheuristics based on tabu search.

- *Parallel Implementation*
  Garcia et al. (1994) apply tabu search to solve the vehicle routing problem with time windows for the first time and describe a parallel implementation of tabu search. By exploring the larger fraction of the search space, parallelism is exploited to produce good solutions within reasonable computational effort.
- *Reactive Tabu Search Heuristics*
  Chiang and Russell (1997) developed a reactive tabu search heuristic. The size of the tabu list varies dynamically to avoid cyclic solutions. To obtain solutions with higher quality, different intensification and diversification strategies have been examined.
- *Post-Optimization Techniques*
  The application of post-optimization techniques is very common for tabu search heuristics. For instance, Cordeau et al. (2001) introduced a unified tabu search heuristic. After a predetermined number of iterations, the best found solution is post-optimized by a specialized heuristic. The heuristic is applied to each tour separately by assuming a traveling salesman problem with time windows and was first introduced by Gendreau et al. (1998).

Generally, multiple approaches to find an initial solution for the tabu search heuristic have been developed in recent years. Also, the algorithms to improve the initial solutions by exploring different neighboring solutions have been studied.

Evolutionary Metaheuristics
Genetic algorithms and evolutionary strategies are both evolutionary metaheuristics. In the following, we will shortly review the most common approaches to solve the vehicle routing problem with time windows.

- *Genetic Algorithms*

  Genetic algorithms are based on population genetics. Thangiah (1995) was among the first to apply genetic algorithms to the vehicle routing problem with time windows. A cluster-first/route-second heuristics was developed. The approach is based on a global customer clustering method and a local post-optimization method. In the clustering step, vehicles are assigned to customers by a search strategy based on population genetics. The best solution found is then improved by a local post-optimization method.

- *Evolutions Strategies*

  Homberger and Gehring (1999) developed two evolutionary metaheuristics for the vehicle routing problem with time windows by applying evolutionary strategies. Similar to genetic algorithms, the basic idea of evolutionary strategies is the manipulation of populations of individuals, which represent solutions of the underlying problem. The main difference to genetic algorithm is the representation of the problem and the search operators. For instance, genetic algorithms encode individuals, but evolutions strategies simulate the process directly on the level of problem solutions.

  Gehring and Homberger (1999) developed a parallel hybrid evolutionary metaheuristic and parallelized a two-phase procedural approach. In the first phase, the number of vehicles are minimized by a $(1,\lambda)$-evolutionary strategy based on Rechenberg (1973). In the second phase, the total distance traveled is minimized by a tabu search approach. By parallelizing, the generation of good solutions for larger problem instances is aspired.

The application of evolutionary metaheuristics requires an initial population. The appropriate approaches use random populations or apply modifications of construction heuristics. Also different selection methods to select a pair for recombinations have been developed in recent years (Bräysy and Gendreau (2005b)). The authors also give a survey on recombination methods ślich as crossover procedures. Finally, mutation schemes are applied in several evolutionary metaheuristics to escape from local optima.

Other Metaheuristics

Besides tabu search methods and evolutionary metaheuristics, multiple other metaheuristics have been used to solve the vehicle routing problem with time windows. The following section describes several of these heuristics in accordance to the work of Bräysy and Gendreau (2005b).

- *Two-Phase Greedy Randomized Adaptive Search Procedure*

  The approach of Kontoravdis and Bard (1995) starts with the initialization of tours. The first customers included into a tour are either the most geographically dispersed or the most time constrained. After initialization, the first phase of the heuristic starts with the main routing algorithm. The routing algorithm identifies the best feasible insertion location for each customer in each tour. In the second phase, a local search tries to find a local optimum. To keep computational effort within acceptable limits, local search is applied to the best found solution after five iterations of the first phase.

- *Neutral Network Procedure*

  The general approach of Potvin and Robillard (1995) is the improvement of the initialization phase of a parallel tour construction heuristic (Antes and Derigs (1995)) by a competitive neutral network model.

- *Simulated Trading Approach*

  The modular simulated trading approach of Bachem et al. (1996) searches for complex customer interchanges to improve an initial solution. The approach is based on the general simulated trading heuristic. The general idea is the application of trading customers between tours to optimize the partition of customers into tours.

- *Simulated Annealing Approaches*

  For the vehicle routing problem with time windows, several simulated annealing based approaches have been developed.

  Chiang and Russell (1996) apply simulated annealing metaheuristics to a parallel construction approach developed by Russell (1995), i.e., improvement and construction procedures are combined.

Li (2003) introduced a metaheuristic based on simulated annealing restarts to diversify and intensify local searches.

A two-stage hybrid algorithm developed by Bent and Van Hentenryck (2004) minimizes the number of vehicles by simulated annealing. In a second step, the total cost is minimized by a large neighborhood search that relocates a large number of customers.

- *Hybrid Search Strategy*
  Thangiah (1999) developed a hybrid search strategy that combines genetic algorithms, simulated annealing and tabu search approaches. First, an initial solution is generated by genetic algorithms. Then, a customer interchange method is used to improve the initial solution. Tabu search in combination with simulated annealing guides the customer interchange method. An evaluation function is applied to penalize the acceptance of infeasible solutions.

- *Guided Local Search Approach*
  Kilby et al. (1999) applied a guided local search to solve the vehicle routing problem with time windows. Guided local search is explained in detail in Voudouris et al. (2010). The approach is a penalty based metaheuristic, i.e., the idea is to add a penalty factor to the objective function to penalize a search, if it ranges too close to previously identified local optima.

- *Route-Neighborhood Based Heuristic*
  The two-stage metaheuristic of Liu (1999) is based on a special neighborhood construction with focus on the relationship between tours and nodes. Tours are constructed in a nested manner to achieve a high solution quality.

- *Ant Colony Optimization Approach*
  The approach applied by Gambardella et al. (1999) is based on a hierarchy of artificial ant colonies. The colonies are designed with a first colony that minimizes the number of vehicles and a second colony that minimizes

the total distance traveled. The colonies are connected by exchanging information via pheromone updating.

- *Constraint-Based Operators*
  Rousseau et al. (2002) used operators that search large neighborhoods to solve the vehicle routing problem with time windows. Pruning and propagation techniques of constraint programming are applied for this approach. By combining the operators in a variable neighborhood descent, the heuristic takes advantage of the different neighborhood structures.
- *Four-Phase Deterministic Heuristics*
  The work of Bräysy (2003) is based on the variable neighborhood search of Mladenovic and Hansen (1997). First, a tour construction heuristic determines an initial solution. Second, the number of vehicles is reduced by a tour elimination procedure. Third, four local search procedures minimize the total distance traveled. Finally, the objective function is modified to escape from the local minimum of the best found solution. The approach is adapted by Bräysy (2004) with modified construction and improvement heuristics.

2.3.2.2 Exact Algorithms for Non-Integer Solutions

Several exact algorithms exist for solving the vehicle routing problem with time windows by relaxing the integrality constraints (2.41) to $x_{ijv} \in [0,1]$. The relaxed problem is easier to solve and provides lower bounds for the integer solutions of the problem. Solution approaches include, for instance, Lagrangian relaxation-based methods, dynamic programming, and column generation. We will follow the description of Larsen (1999) and Cordeau et al. (2002) to represent an overview of different approaches.

Lagrangian Relaxation-Based Methods Based on Lagrangian relaxation, several solution approaches for the vehicle routing problem with time windows have been developed. We briefly review the variable splitting, the K-tree and the shortest path with side constraints approach.

Variable Splitting Approach

The variable splitting approach by Fisher et al. (1997) applies Lagrangian relaxation by splitting variables into multiple copies. This results in a decomposition of the problem into a number of independent subproblems. In Equations (2.33) - (2.41), a new decision variable γ_{iv} is introduced and is defined as follows (Larsen (1999)):

$$\sum_{j \in V \setminus \{0\}} x_{ijv} = \gamma_{iv} \quad \forall i \in V \setminus \{n+1\}, \forall v \in VE, \tag{2.42}$$

with $\gamma_{iv} = 1$, if vehicle v includes customer i and with $\gamma_{iv} = 0$, if vehicle v does not include customer i.

Some of the constraints of Equations (2.33) - (2.41) are reformulated by using the decision variables γ_{iv} instead of x_{ijv}. Then, the coupling condition (Constraints (2.42)) is Lagrangian relaxed and the resulting subproblem is decomposed into two subproblem, one in the γ_{iv} variables, one in the flow, time and capacity variables (Cordeau et al. (2002)).

K-Tree Relaxation Approach

The K-tree approach of Fisher et al. (1997) is an extension of the 1-tree approach that was introduced by Held and Karp (1970, 1971) to solve the traveling salesman problem with capacity constrained vehicles. The corresponding approach assumes that each tour covers a minimum of two customers. By a Lagrangian relaxation of the flow conversation, capacity and time constraints, a degree constrained K-tree problem is generated. The use of the subgradient method determines the Lagrangian multipliers. New constraints are generated as they are violated.

Shortest Path with Side Constraints Approach

The method of Kohl and Madsen (1997) relaxes the covering constraints (2.33), i.e., that every customer has to be visited exactly once. The resulting master problem consists of finding the optimal Lagrangian multiplier and the subproblem results in a shortest path problem with time windows and capacity constraints. Exploiting the benefits of subgradient and using a bundle approach, the Lagrangian multipliers are determined.

Dynamic Programming Kolen et al. (1987) were the first to present a dynamic programming approach for the vehicle routing problem with time windows. The approach is partially inspired by the dynamic programming approach of Christofides et al. (1981) who provided a state space relaxation algorithm to reduce the state space. Kolen et al. (1987) used a different implementation of this approach.

The branch-and-bound method of Kolen et al. (1987) includes the following branching rule: Each node α of the search tree is connected to a set $F(\alpha)$ of fixed tours with start and end at depot, a set $P(\alpha)$ of partial tours with start at the depot, and a set $C(\alpha)$ of customers that are forbidden to be next on $P(\alpha)$. At the beginning, it holds that, $F(\alpha)$ and $C(\alpha)$ are empty sets, but $P(\alpha)$ includes only the depot.

The branching step starts with the selection of a customer i. The customer i is neither part of set $F(\alpha)$ nor of set $P(\alpha)$ and the customer is not forbidden. The selection process is performed with a selection heuristic. By branching two new nodes, α' and α'' are created. The partial route $P(\alpha)$ is extended by i in α'. In α", i is forbidden as next customer.

At each node α of the search tree, a lower bound on all possible feasible solutions characterized by $F(\alpha)$, $P(\alpha)$, and $C(\alpha)$ is determined by dynamic programming. The general idea is to relax the condition that each client not yet on a route must be served exactly once.

Column Generation The vehicle routing problem with time windows can be solved optimally using column generation. As the column generation approach is implemented as part of the solution approaches of this thesis, a comprehensive overview will be presented in Chapter 3.

2.3.2.3 Exact Integer Solutions

To obtain an integer optimal solution of the vehicle routing problem with time windows, a common approach is to make branching and cutting decisions on the binary decision variables (Cordeau et al. (2002)). The decomposition process that involves Lagrangian relaxation or column generation is repeated at each branching node. Either binary or integer decisions on arc flow variables can be made. Also binary decisions on path flow variables are presented. Finally, Cordeau et al. (2002) report subtour elimination and 2-path cuts, as well as multiple-path cuts and parallelism, and integer decisions on time variables to decide on branching and cutting.

In Chapter 3, we will give a comprehensive survey of branch-and-bound in combination with column generation, because this so-called branch-and-price approach will be implemented for this thesis.

2.3.3 Conclusion

For the vehicle routing problem with time windows, we presented multiple heuristic and exact solution approaches. The problem is more difficult to solve than the vehicle routing problem. Therefore, exact methods are not often applied to very large-scale and complex problem instances. Again, heuristic solution approaches are preferred, because these approaches already provide a good solution quality. Metaheuristics are very popular due to their flexibility and simplicity. These are, for instance, tabu search, and simulated annealing approaches (Cordeau et al. (2002)).

2.4 Crew Scheduling Problem

2.4.1 Problem Description

The service routing problem with fixed delivery times can be formulated as a crew scheduling problem. In this section, we will present this class of problems.

The crew scheduling problem has the objective to find the cost minimal crew schedule that covers all activities, i.e., it deals with the assignment of crews to a given set of activities. For that purpose, duties, i.e., a sequence of activities, are built under the assumption that each duty can be fulfilled by one crew with respect to applicable constraints. These constraints can be given, for instance, by legal regulations that limit the maximum work time of each crew. Other constraints can be defined by operational requirements such as robustness that ensures the accordance between planning and practical execution. The literature on crew scheduling deals mainly with the solution of a crew scheduling problem in a specific context. Best known is the research in the airline crew scheduling. The most notable survey contributions on airline crew scheduling are Etschmaier and Mathaisel (1985), Desaulniers et al. (1998b), Desrosiers et al. (1995), Barnhart et al. (2003), and Gopalakrishnan and Johnson (2005). Examples for the mass transit scheduling problem are provided, for instance, by Guihaire and Hao (2008) and Wren and Rousseau (1995). In the area of railway crew scheduling, Ernst et al. (2001) give an extensive review of optimization algorithms. Passenger railway optimization is presented by Caprara et al. (2007), but models, methods, and applications for freight railway crew scheduling were most recently provided by Albers (2009). For a general overview of crew scheduling problems, Ernst et al. (2004) provide a compact survey on relevant approaches.

In the following, we assume that the crew scheduling problem focuses on generating daily schedules, in most literature referred to as crew pairing problem (Barnhart et al. (2003)).

2.4.2 Solution Approaches

In this section, we will shortly review traditional approaches to solve the crew scheduling problem by presenting the two main approaches: run-cutting approaches and matching based algorithms (Qiao et al. (2010)). Then, we will focus on the most common approaches that are usually based on set partitioning formulations (Gopalakrishnan and Johnson (2005)).

2.4.2.1 Traditional Solution Approaches

Run-Cutting Approaches Bodin et al. (1983) refer to the general set of heuristic approaches used by manual schedulers as run-cutting heuristics. The approach is a constructive method to cover all duties successively (Cavique et al. (1999)).

We use the notation of Bodin et al. (1983) to illustrate run-cutting approaches. The algorithm is performed in two steps. In a first step, the algorithm cuts trip blocks into crew work periods, so-called pieces of work. Blocks specify the work plan for vehicles. Then, two or three pieces of work are combined to build a feasible duty, so-called run. If all pieces of work are covered, i.e., a run is assigned to each piece of work, the process terminates and results in an initial feasible crew schedule. In a second step, the crew schedule is optimized by improving runs. The improvement is done by modifying the cuts of the blocks into pieces of work or by exchanging pieces of works between different runs.

Cavique et al. (1999) provide two extensions of the run-cutting approach, a tabu search and an ejection chain based approach. The first approach embeds the run-cutting method into a tabu search framework. After the determination of an initial schedule, a predetermined number of runs are removed from the schedule. Next, the run-cutting algorithm generates new runs to cover all resulting uncovered pieces of work.

The second approach of Cavique et al. (1999) is based on ejection chains, a local search approach. The algorithm applies moves using a subgraph ejection chain method. Ejection chain methods evaluate a neighborhood of a solution by successive transformations of one structure into another structure. In most cases, the structure represents a partially disconnected or incomplete solution, but allows evaluating the trial solution of each step of the ejection chain. After the determination of the best trial solution, the method performs a move that connects the current solution subgraph and generates a complete solution.

Matching Based Algorithms The approach is based on a reduced crew scheduling graph. The nodes of the graph represent d-trips. A d-trip is a portion of a trip a single crew must perform. A piece is the part of the crew schedule in which the crew remains on the same vehicle. A run consists of multiple pieces that form a schedule for a single crew. The solution process is divided into three components: a piece construction, a piece improvement, and a run generation component (Ball et al. (1983)).

Piece Construction

The approach starts by partitioning the nodes in the reduced crew scheduling graph into paths. The path lengths are restricted. The length of a path is defined by the number of arcs. Each node of the graph is associated with a level that equals the length of the longest path from the start node of the graph to the corresponding node. Figure 2.3 illustrates the partitioning of nodes into levels (Ball et al. (1983)). In each iteration, the pieces are enlarged and the nodes

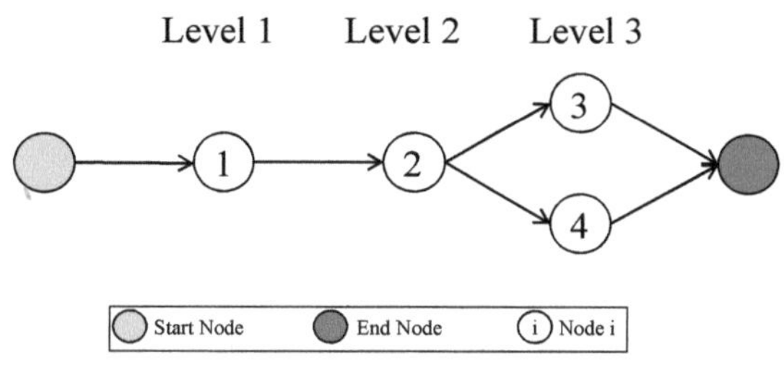

Figure 2.3: Partition of Nodes into Levels

are added on the next higher numbered level of the graph. If possible, the algorithm merges theses nodes into already generated pieces. If it is not possible to merge the nodes, the corresponding node forms the beginning of a new piece. To find the optimal set of merges, the problem is formulated and solved as a matching problem. A matching problem is a set partitioning problem with columns containing not more than two pieces.

Piece Improvement

After the construction of pieces in the construction component, the algorithm tries to improve the solution by combining and resplitting pairs of pieces. The arranging of pieces can be performed in three different ways. The first possibility is the combination of two short pieces into a larger piece. The second option is the combination of a short and a large piece and the resplitting of them in two pieces of moderate length. The third option is the combination of two pieces and the resplitting into other pieces to eliminate a trip to the end node. For the arrangement of pieces, each possible combination split is associated with a cost that is based on a piece function. Then, a matching problem is solved to find the minimum cost set of combinations and/or splits. The process is repeated until no more improvements can be found.

Run Generation
The last phase of the matching based algorithm combines pieces found by the improvement phase into runs. The algorithm starts with the combination of pairings of pieces into partial runs. Then, the final set of runs is determined based on the solution of a matching algorithm. The final set of runs consists either of two partial runs, two pieces, or a partial run and a piece.

The literature on crew scheduling problem provides additional matching based algorithms (Qiao et al. (2010)). Martello and Toth (1986) introduce a greedy heuristic. The approach extends feasible partial solutions based on the solutions of multiple matching problems. Ball and Benoit-Thompson (1988) present another matching based algorithm by decomposing the crew scheduling problem into a shortest path problem and a matching problem. Based on this decomposition, the algorithm iterates between the solutions of both problems. The consideration of Lagrangian penalties associated with adequate subgraph inequalities derives the objective function value of the shortest path problem. The matching problem generates runs consisting of one or two pieces.

2.4.2.2 Most Common Approaches

To present the most common approaches in crew scheduling, we follow the work of Gopalakrishnan and Johnson (2005). The core of the crew scheduling problem is usually a set partitioning problem (Barnhart et al. (2003)): Let I be the set of all activities at different locations to be covered and J the set of all feasible duties. Each duty $j \in J$ is associated with cost c_j. Then, the problem is formulated as follows:

$$\min \quad \sum_{j \in J} c_j x_j \tag{2.43}$$

$$s.t. \quad \sum_{j \in J} a_{ij} x_j = 1 \qquad \forall i \in I \tag{2.44}$$

$$x_j \in \{0,1\} \qquad \forall j \in J. \tag{2.45}$$

x_j is the decision variable and indicates whether duty j is part of the solution ($x_j = 1$) or not ($x_j = 0$). The parameter a_{ij} is equal to 1, if activity i is part of duty j and 0, otherwise.

The determination of the set of feasible duties J can be based on three different approaches, row approach, column approach, and network approach. Rows denote activities and columns represent duties.

Row Approach

The row approach is described as an approach that applies local optimization to an initial feasible solution of the crew scheduling problem. Then, a certain number of duties is chosen from the current solution. The algorithm forms a subproblem consisting of all possible duties that cover all activities of the chosen solution. In a next step, the approach determines an integer solution to the set partitioning problem. The resulting integer solution cannot be worse than the old solution of the subproblem and therefore it is kept for the next iteration. The process restarts by selecting new duties and continues until a certain stopping criterion is met.

Column Approach

In the column approach, the generation of duties in the subproblem considers all rows simultaneously. For large problem-instances, column generation is applied to avoid the generation of all feasible duties by generating candidate duties. Then, the subproblem is solved optimally and a new subproblem with a better objective value is determined for the next iteration. The process restarts and continues until the optimal solution is found.

Network Approach

The network approach formulates problems including vehicle movement as routing problems in graphs. Generally, the nodes are associated to locations and the arcs to the connections between the locations. The length of an arc indicates the cost for choosing the appropriate connection. The network approach is similar to the column approach and generates columns by using the duty network.

An explicit enumeration can identify all feasible duties to solve the set partitioning problem (2.43) - (2.45). But Barnhart et al. (2003) state three reasons for the difficulty of determining all duties. First, the decision whether a sequence of activities is feasible is difficult to make due to given rules and regulations that must be enforced. Second, the problem consists usually of a high number of variables. Third, the claim of integer variables complicates the solution process. Consequently, the following solution approaches for large-instance problems generate duties without explicitly enumerating all:

TPACS/TRIP Approaches

The trip pairing for airline crew scheduling (TRACS) developed by Rubin (1973) is described as a creative solution approach. Trip pairings denote round-trip sequences of activities. The idea is to extract multiple small set covering problems from the original problem and to solve them by a good solution approach. The objective is to produce a series of small improvements to the original problem (Rubin (1973)).

Based on TPACS, the trip (re)-evaluation and improvement program (TRIP) has been developed. The approach builds on iteratively improving the duties by generating and solving multiple subproblems (Anbil et al. (1991)). The objective of the TRIP enhancements includes the increase of TRIP iteration speed, the improvement of duty generation, and the solution of larger subproblems.

Linear Programming Approaches

In the following, we present two common linear programming algorithms as examples for rapid solution approaches (Gopalakrishnan and Johnson (2005)).

- *SPRINT*

  SPRINT is a method introduced by Forrest (1989) to solve linear programming problems quickly. The approach generates the optimal solution of a crew scheduling problem by considering a sequence of smaller linear programs.

  First, only a subset of feasible duties is chosen. Then, a linear program is solved with this subset of columns. The resulting dual variables help to identify columns with negative reduced cost. If no columns with negative reduced cost exist, the current solution is optimal. Otherwise, the process restarts by adding columns with negative reduced cost close to zero to the subproblem. It continues until no more columns with negative reduced cost are found.

- *Volume Algorithm*

  Barahona and Anbil (2000) introduce the volume algorithm as an extension of a subgradient algorithm to determine primal and dual solutions. The approach quickly approximates the Dantzig-Wolfe decomposition and provides approximations for large-scale linear programs.

Integer Programming Approaches

To obtain a good integer solution to the crew scheduling problem, the application of traditional branch-and-bound approaches to the entire problem is almost impossible (Gopalakrishnan and Johnson (2005)). As the use of a subset of columns may also not be beneficial, multiple heuristics have been developed. First, we report branching rules that are crucial for solving large-scale problem instances. Then, we describe branch-and-cut and branch-and-price approaches.

- *Branching*

  The *follow-on branching* was first introduced by Foster and Ryan (1981). The follow-on is the second activity of consecutive activities i and j covered by a duty, i.e., activity j. In one branch, activities i and j have to be consecutively in all duties. In the other branch, the two are not allowed to appear consecutively.

The *timeline branching* developed by Klabjan et al. (2001) is based on the follow-on branching rule and on the SOS branching of Beale and Tomlin (1970). The general idea is to order the set of J_i of all duties covering activity i by their connection time with activity i. Then, the approach assigns weights to the connection time. Based on the weights, it is decided which activities are fixed.

Klabjan et al. (2001) enhance the approach by *strong branching*. Strong branching enables to choose a good branching pair for the previous branching approaches. For each possible branching candidate, two branches are formed and the objective values of the branches are determined. Based on the values, the next branching candidate is chosen.

- *Branch-and-Cut*

  We base our description of branch-and-cut on the work of Hoffman and Padberg (1993). They design a branch-and-cut optimizer to solve large set partitioning problems. First, a lower bound is determined by optimizing the LP-relaxation by a linear programming. Second, an upper bound is obtained by a linear programming based heuristic. To fix variables, the *reduced cost fixing* procedure of Crowder et al. (1983) is applied. If no variables can be fixed, the constraint generation phase is started. The constraints are based on polyhedral theory and are referred to as polyhedral cuts.

- *Branch-and-Price*

  The branch-and-price approach is similar to the branch-and-cut approach. Branch-and-price focuses on pricing or dynamically generating columns instead of constraint generation as in branch-and-cut. Approaches for the crew scheduling problem have been proposed, for instance, by Barnhart et al. (1998a).

Since one part of this thesis deals with the scheduling of personnel, column generation and branch-and-price are described in detail in Chapter 3.

Parallel Computing

The use of parallel computing improves significantly the computational power of optimization tools. A detailed description of parallelism at the hardware level is provided by Gendron and Crainic (1994). It is required that parts of the optimization problem do not have to be solved in sequence, but can be solved independently from each other. Particularly, branch-and-bound as well as branch-and-cut-and-price techniques have been efficiently parallelized (Gendron and Crainic (1994), Ralphs et al. (2001)).

Gendron and Crainic (1994) propose three main methods to parallelize branch-and-bound algorithms: *Type 1* applies parallelism in the process of generating subproblems. Gendron and Crainic (1994) state that the type of parallelism has no influence on the structure of the branch-and-bound approach. *Type 2* parallelizes the building of the branch-and-bound tree, i.e., the subproblems are performed simultaneously. The structure of the branch-and-bound tree algorithm may be affected. *Type 3* builds multiple branch-and-bound trees in parallel. The different types of parallelism can be combined.

Ralphs et al. (2001) apply a branch-and-cut-and-price approach. Branch-and-cut-and-price approaches solve large-scale discrete optimization problems. The general idea is the dynamic generation of both variables and constraints during LP-based branch-and-bound. The parallelism can be based on two main sources. The first source is the simultaneous processing of subproblem groups on the current candidate list. The second source is the parallelism of processing individual subproblems.

Gopalakrishnan and Johnson (2005) give a survey on further parallel techniques to solve the crew scheduling problem. They state that the parallel pairing generation developed by Klabjan and Schwan (2001) can also be combined with branch-and-price approaches.

Other Approaches

In the following, we shortly present an approximation approach and alternate formulations to solve the crew scheduling problem.

- *Approximation Approach*

  Another efficient solution approach for the crew scheduling problem is the approximation algorithm of Wedelin (1995) for solving large 0-1 integer programming problems. The approach is based on a dual coordinate search for solving the LP-relaxation. Additionally, an approximation scheme is applied to the approach by adjusting the cost as little as possible to find an integer solution of the new problem. A parameter determines the degree of approximation.

- *Alternate Formulations*

  Besides the set partitioning formulation, Gopalakrishnan and Johnson (2005) report other formulations for solving the crew scheduling problem. In the following, we shortly review the integer nonlinear multi-commodity network flow formulation and the duty-based formulation of the crew scheduling problem.

  Desaulniers (1997) formulate the crew scheduling problem as integer nonlinear multi-commodity network flow model with additional resource variables. The model handles possible nonlinearities in the objective function and in a large subset of constraints. The model is solved by a branch-and-bound approach based on an extension to the Dantzig-Wolfe decomposition principle (Dantzig and Wolfe (1960)). The master problem is formulated as set partitioning model. The characteristic of the approach of Desaulniers (1997) is the generation of duties by shortest path subproblems with resource constraints. In the approach, all feasible duties are implicitly considered. Additionally, the optimality gap value on a feasible solution is determined.

  Vance et al. (1997) describe a *duty-based formulation*. The formulation is applicable if not only duties are generated that are based on a single workday. The approach is applied to problems that generate pairings, i.e., sequences of duties with overnight rests. The model of Vance et al. (1997) is based on dividing the decision into two stages. In the first stage, a set of duties is selected to cover all activities. In the second stage, pairings are built based on the duties. A decomposition approach is presented to solve the model.

2.4.3 Conclusion

For the crew scheduling problem, we described traditional and most common solution approaches. We saw that branch-and-price is a powerful approach to solve multiple problems optimally within acceptable time. Only for very large-problem instances, branch-and-price is combined with heuristics, like variable fixing procedures, to speed up the solution process.

2.5 Inventory Routing Problem

2.5.1 Problem Description

The inventory routing problem combines inventory and routing decisions. Similar to the service routing problem, the inventory routing problem can decide on the delivery times. The characteristic is that the deliveries must be fulfilled before the customers run out of inventory. In most cases, vehicle load and inventory capacities have to be considered.

Campbell et al. (1998) describe the inventory routing problem as the manifold distribution of a product, to several retailers, from a single depot, and over a given planning horizon H. The retailers are usually delivered by a homogeneous fleet of vehicles. Each retailer consumes the product with a given rate and can stock the product. The objective is usually the minimization of total cost without causing any stock-outs. In the following, we present the general inventory problem in accordance to Schwarz et al. (2004).

Schwarz et al. (2004) indicate the inventory policy by vector θ and the transportation policy by ϖ. $C_t(\theta,\varpi)$ denote the cost of period t. Then, the general inventory problem can be formulated as follows:

$$\begin{aligned} \min \quad & \sum_{t=0}^{H} C_t(\theta, \varpi) && (2.46) \\ s.t. \quad & \theta \in \Omega && (2.47) \\ & \varpi \in \Pi. && (2.48) \end{aligned}$$

The objective is the minimization of the total cost over the planning horizon (2.46). Equations (2.47) and (2.48) indicate that the inventory policy has to be chosen from a given set Ω and the transportation policy from a given set Π.

2.5.2 Solution Approaches

There exist a large body of settings and many different solution approaches for the inventory routing problem. The literature considers single period models (e.g., Dror et al. (1985), Chien et al. (1989)), multiple period models with periodic schedules (e.g., Bertazzi et al. (2002), Alegre et al. (2007)), and multiple period models with non-periodic schedules (e.g., Carter et al. (1996), Campbell and Savelsbergh (2004)). Due to the complexity of the inventory routing problem, it is difficult to provide an optimal solution approach (Andersson et al. (2010)). Exact methods generally do not solve a problem within acceptable computational time. Therefore, the solution process terminates after a predetermined solution time. Often, heuristics and metaheuristics are used.

In the following, we will present the most common solution approaches considering the sum of transportation and inventory costs, and approaches considering only transportation cost.

2.5.2.1 Inventory and Transportation Costs

We assume that costs consist of inventory cost and transportation cost and the objective is to find a delivery schedule that minimizes the sum of both. To our best knowledge, no good exact solution approach is present for the case considering both cost factors. In the following, we will therefore focus on the most common heuristic solution approaches.

Fixed Partitioning Policies

To determine replenishment strategies that minimize transportation and inventory holding costs, retailers are divided into several regions referred to as clusters (Andersson et al. (2010)). If a retailer of a specific cluster receives a delivery, the delivering vehicle visits all other retailers of the cluster as well, i.e., each cluster is served independently from the other cluster. If a retailer belongs to multiple clusters, the retailer is served partially by each cluster.

Anily and Federgruen (1990) consider a distribution system with a single depot and multiple retailers. The retailers are divided into non-disjoint clusters. The demand rate at each retailer is the multiple of a given value. This characteristic is used to decide on the choice of clusters, i.e., based on so-called demand points, the partitioning is performed. Allowing the depot to hold inventory, Anily and Federgruen (1993) extend the model of Anily and Federgruen (1990) and adapt the solution approach.

The model of Chan et al. (1998) considers a distribution system with a fleet of vehicles with limited capacities that depart from a single depot. To minimize the infinite horizon cost, a combined inventory and routing policy is applied. A close-to optimal fixed partitioning policy is developed.

Anily and Bramel (2004) assume a fixed partitioning policy based on Anily and Federgruen (1990). The retailers are divided into disjoint sets, i.e., each retailer belongs to only one cluster. The set of retailers is then served at its optimal replenishment rate.

Aghezzaf et al. (2006) also considers distribution and inventory holding costs. The work proposes a model with stable demand rates and applies economic-order quantity based policies. A column generation approach is used to solve the nonlinear integer formulation of the problem. A saving-based heuristic solves the subproblems. The solution approach allows constructing optimal partitions of the retailers.

Zhao et al. (2007) combine a fixed partitioning policy and tabu-search. The replenishment interval of each cluster is based on the so-called power-of-two principle. The general power-of-two principle replenishes the retailers when the inventory reaches zero. By tabu search, the optimal partition regions are determined.

Mixed Integer Programming Models

Bell et al. (1983) consider inventory management for industrial gases in combination with vehicle scheduling and dispatching. The vehicles have constrained capacities. A mathematical optimization tool produces daily schedules by using a Lagrangian relaxation approach to solve a mixed integer program.

The model of Chien et al. (1989) is based on the distribution of a limited amount of inventory to retailers by a capacitated fleet of vehicles with the objective to maximize profit. Chien et al. (1989) formulate the problem as a mixed integer program and develop a Lagrangian relaxation procedure to determine good upper bounds and heuristic solutions. For a given set of Lagrangian multipliers, the problem is decomposed into an inventory allocation subproblem and a retailer assignment subproblem.

The approach of Campbell et al. (1998) is a two-phase approach that determines when and how much to deliver in the first phase. In the second phase, delivery rates are determined for the given delivery quantities and times. The authors apply a fixed partitioning policy by building disjoint clusters covering all retailers.

Decomposition Approaches

Federgruen and Zipkin (1984) consider a model that balances inventory carrying and shortage costs, and also considers transportation cost. The problem is formulated as a mathematical programming model. The model is partially separated into subproblems to be able to apply interchange heuristics developed for the vehicle routing problem.

The model of Qu (1999) considers the replenishment of multiple products with a stochastic demand rate. The approach is based on a modified periodic-review inventory policy and traveling salesman problem component. The problem is heuristically solved by decomposing the problem into separate inventory and routing decisions. Then, the approach iterates between both problems to solve the overall model.

Dynamic Programming Approaches

For a stochastic demand rate, Campbell et al. (1998) model the inventory routing problem as a discrete Markov decision process. After the determination of the inventory of each retailer at the beginning of each day, it is decided which retailers to serve, how much to deliver, how to combine retailers to tours and how to assign tours to vehicles.

Kleywegt et al. (2002) consider the inventory routing problem with a stochastic demand rate and direct deliveries, i.e., only one retailer is replenished by a vehicle trip. The problem is modeled as a Markov decision process. The value function is approximated based on the decomposition of the problem into individual retailer subproblems.

Kleywegt et al. (2004) extend the model of Kleywegt et al. (2002) allowing multiple deliveries per vehicle trip. The problem is also formulated as a Markov decision process and the dynamic programming value function is approximated using decomposition and optimization. The problem is decomposed into subproblems that are easier to solve than the overall problem. The solutions of the subproblems are combined defining an optimization problem whose objective function value approximates the value of a given state of the process.

Genetic Algorithms

Abdelmaguid and Dessouky (2006) and Dauzere-Peres et al. (2007) use a genetic algorithm to solve inventory routing problems.

Besides inventory and transportation costs, Abdelmaguid and Dessouky (2006) considers backorder penalty cost. The approach combines a construction heuristic with a genetic algorithm and decomposes the inventory routing problem into an inventory and a routing problem. Based on a construction heuristic, an initial random solution is generated. In the improvement phase, crossover and mutation operators are designed.

Dauzere-Peres et al. (2007) apply inventory routing in a maritime context, i.e., trips from a plant to tank farms are planned to minimize transportation and inventory costs. The optimization is based on genetic algorithm that combines local search and crossover operators. In a first step, a greedy heuristic determines the delivery schedules for the tank farms based on a given fixed tank farm order. Then, the solution is improved by swapping tank farms in the fixed order. To explore the solution space, a genetic algorithm is applied with a tank farm order as chromosome. Different crossover and mutation operators are used to obtain a good solution.

Construction and Insertion Heuristics
Savelsbergh and Song (2007) apply a greedy construction heuristic to solve an inventory routing problem with continuous moves, i.e., product pickups are involved. Instead of using a delivery schedule for each retailer, only the next visit to each retailer is considered. Delivery decisions are made based on an index that indicates the urgency of deliver to a certain retailer. After the construction of a schedule, the delivery volumes are optimized.

Viswanathan and Mathur (1997) focus on a distribution system with one warehouse and retailers stocking multiple products. A stationary nested joint replenishment policy is developed that solves a problem with multiple products. A stationary approach applies constant replenishment intervals. A nested policy indicates that the replenishment intervals of the problems are multipliers of each other. Power-of-two principles are applied to decide on the replenishment intervals. A modified insertion heuristic is used to solve the traveling salesman problem in the stationary nested joint replenishment policy.

2.5.2.2 Transportation Cost

Some literature on inventory routing considers only transportation cost. The models are applied in settings where the retailer owns the inventory and inventory cost is not relevant to the decision makers. However, inventory capacities and possible stockouts at the customers still have to be considered. The structure of an optimal policy is known only for small problem instances, e.g., for the single-retailer problem. The majority of the literature deals with heuristic solution approaches. In the following, we review the most common solution approaches.

Exact Solution Approaches

Single-Retailer Problem

To our best knowledge, optimal solution approaches are only known for the single-retailer problem by ignoring future periods. Dror and Ball (1987) assume a deterministic single-retailer model with events occurring on continuous time. The retailer has to refill customer's oil tanks without causing any stock-outs. For a single retailer the optimal replenishment time is when the tank reaches its zero level. Assuming a fix tank size of F, a daily demand rate of μ, a cost c_{refill} for refilling the tank, and an opening inventory of I_0, the continuous approximation of the cost over n days is

$$\frac{c_{refill}(n\mu - I_0)}{F}.$$

Other Small-Scale Problem Instances

Christiansen (1999) presents a real ship planning problem that involves an inventory management problem and a vehicle routing problem with time windows. A single product is shipped from multiple depots to multiple retailers. The problem is decomposed based on a Dantzig-Wolfe decomposition approach with ship routing subproblems and inventory management subproblems. Using branch-and-bound, the overall problem is solved. Due to the great computational effort of large-scale problem instances, the process terminates after a predetermined time.

The model of Alkhayyal and Hwang (2007) is also based on a ship planning problem. The heterogeneous fleet of ships delivers multiple products from multiple depots to multiple retailers. The problem is formulated as a mixed integer nonlinear program that can be reformulated as a mixed integer linear program with special structure. Similar to Christiansen (1999), the problem is not solved to optimality for large-scale problem instances, but the algorithm is terminated after a certain time is elapsed.

Heuristic Solution Approaches

Decomposition Approaches

Carter et al. (1996) decompose the inventory routing problem into two phases and embed it in a rolling-horizon framework. In the first phase, an allocation problem is solved and in the second phase, a routing problem is optimized. Carter et al. (1996) use a capacitated allocation problem in the first phase to determine the quantity of a product to be delivered to each customer. In the second phase, the routing problem is modeled as a vehicle routing problem with time windows and solved heuristically to identify delivery tours. If the vehicle routing problem with time windows results in an infeasible solution, the capacity constraints in the allocation problem are adapted and the problem is resolved.

Bertazzi et al. (2002) examine a problem with multiple products which have to be shipped to several retailers. A ship with fixed transportation capacity transports the products to the retailers. The solution approach is divided into two phases. In the first phase, an iterative procedure inserts a retailer in the solutions based on the cheapest cost. In the second phase, retailers are removed from the solution and are again inserted according to the procedure of the first phase. If costs are reduced, the solution is accepted and the second phase is restarted. The process terminates when no more improvements are found.

Similar to Carter et al. (1996), Campbell and Savelsbergh (2004) also decompose the problem into two phases and consider a rolling-horizon framework. Retailers are assigned to delivery days in the first phase. Based on vehicle capacities, upper and lower bounds for the delivery volume to each retailer are determined. In the second phase, subproblems are formulated as general integer programs. The subproblems are solved by an insertion heuristic to construct delivery routes.

Other Approaches

Dror et al. (1985) and Dror and Ball (1987) develop a reduction and retailer-selection procedure for the needs of a propane-distribution company. It is assumed that a retailer's stock-out can be prevented by emergency deliveries. Although both works focus on an instant time horizon, the long-time effects of short-time actions are considered as future cost. Therefore, fixed cost associated with a delivery to a retailer is expressed as the direct added cost of including this retailer. Then, the problem of minimizing annual distribution cost can be reduced to a problem of optimizing over a small planning horizon. The steps of the proposed algorithm are as follows: In a first step, the approach assigns retailers to days using a linear-programming-based algorithm. Then, the vehicle routing problem is solved heuristically by a saving-based approach. Finally, the solution is improved by exchanging retailers between tours.

Trudeau and Dror (1992) solve the inventory routing problem with stochastic demand rate based on the distribution of heating oil. The problem contains also possible route failures when the demand exceeds the capacity of a vehicle. The solution approach can be divided into four stages. In the first stage, the replenishment day is determined for each retailer. In the second stage, an assignment procedure assigns retailers to days of the planning horizon heuristically. In the third stage, the resulting vehicle routing problems are solved by a saving-based heuristic. In the fourth stage, retailers are exchanged to improve the solution. The algorithm for the third and fourth stage considers explicitly the costs of stock-outs and route failures.

Herer and Roundy (1997) consider a combination of a one warehouse retailer distribution problem with a traveling salesman problem. Polynomial time heuristics are developed to find good solutions. Based on dynamic programming, optimal power-of-two reorder intervals are determined for the problem with general nonnegative monotone order cost.

Hemmelmayr et al. (2008) consider a very specific inventory routing problem based on delivery strategies for blood products and develop three different solution approaches. The first approach delivers blood products to hospitals on the day of stock-out and solves the resulting vehicle routing problem heuristically. The second approach is an integer programming approach and divides the hospitals into regional clusters. The third approach is a variable neighborhood search and considers the inventory routing problem as a periodic vehicle routing problem, i.e., fixed delivery frequencies are specified.

2.5.3 Conclusion

For the inventory routing problem, we showed heuristic and exact solution approaches. Exact solution approaches are rare and most methods are based on heuristic approaches. We saw that the inventory routing problem is often based on a very specific problem instance. Most often, each setting includes its own specific solution approach. Therefore, no clear recommendation on solution approaches can be given. However, the decomposition of the problem into two problems is generally a useful first approach to structure the solution process.

2.6 Summary

We provided a general overview of models and solution approaches for routing and scheduling problems. For the routing problems, the traveling salesman problem, the vehicle routing problem, and the vehicle routing problem with time windows, we saw that the approaches to explore different neighborhood solutions are very common. Local search approaches are applied to determine local optima. These approaches are enhanced by global search heuristics like tabu search and simulated annealing to escape from local optima. Due to their robustness and flexibility, those metaheuristics are useful approaches for the exploration of different service tables of the service routing problem to reduce the overall service routing cost. We describe the general approaches in detail in Chapter 4.

To solve the crew scheduling problem, we showed that branch-and-price is a very common exact solution approach. It provides a good basis for our solution approach to solve the service routing problem with fixed delivery times optimally. Therefore, we review more details on branch-and-price in Chapter 3.

At first sight, the inventory routing problem has many similarities to the service routing problem. Both problems can decide on delivery times with impact on cost and future delivery times. However, most inventory routing problems deal with a specific problem that cannot be easily transferred to other problem formulations. Furthermore, the service routing problem has another objective due to its special problem requirements. The focus of attention of the inventory routing problem is transportation capacities, transportation cost, and inventory cost. The optimization approaches typically take advantage of some special properties of the problem. For instance, the inventory routing problem may allow at most one visit during a day or may use transportation capacities to reduce the search space. In the service routing problem, such special properties cannot be utilized in the optimization algorithms, because locations can require service several times during a day and vehicles are incapacitated. The service routing problem focuses on service personnel and the optimization must ensure that complex work regulations are met, such as break time requirements and minimum duty lengths. Based on these constraints, we can reduce the search space of the service routing problem. But the number of possible solutions remains more complex and requires a reasonable solution approach. Although, the problem characteristics of the inventory routing problem differ from the service routing problem, the decomposition approaches for the inventory routing problem provide a good basis for our solution approaches in Chapter 7.

3 Crew Scheduling Optimization

One challenge of this thesis is the scheduling of service personnel. The corresponding crew scheduling problem can be solved optimally by branch-and-price. We will adapt the branch-and-price algorithm of Barnhart et al. (1998a) and Savelsbergh (2001), which embeds column generation in a branch-and-bound tree.

Section 3.1 defines the important terms for the crew scheduling problem. Section 3.2 divides the crew scheduling problem into two problems: a master problem and a subproblem. The master problem can be formulated as set partitioning or as set covering problem. The subproblem generates duties for the master problem and is formulated as shortest path problem with resource constraints. To solve the shortest path problem with resource constraints, an appropriate network representation has to be chosen. Section 3.3 describes the approaches to solve the master problem and the subproblem. The approaches are based on column generation and dynamic programming. The fundamental basics of the following explanations are given by Albers (2009) and Malcherek (2010).

3.1 Definition of Terms

The crew scheduling problem has its origin in the airline sector and deals mainly with airline or mass transit. In the crew scheduling problem, a *crew* is a group of employees. A *duty* is a sequence of jobs a crew has to perform. The different jobs to be covered by a duty are mostly called *(flight) legs* (Barnhart et al. (1998a), Gopalakrishnan and Johnson (2005)). In the railway crew scheduling the notation *trip* is very common (Caprara et al. (2007)). We use the term *task* following Beasley (1996). The term *activity* is used as synonym for the term task.

N. Holtvogt, *The Service Routing Problem*, Edition KWV,
https://doi.org/10.1007/978-3-658-24126-1_3

The objective of the crew scheduling problem is to find the optimal *crew schedule*, i.e, the construction of a cost minimal set of duties for multiple groups of employees.

3.2 Formulation

The objective of the crew scheduling problem is to find the cost minimal crew schedule that covers all tasks. The problem is decomposed into a master problem and a subproblem. The master problem selects the optimal subset of duties and the subproblem provides a set of feasible duties.

3.2.1 Master Problem

The master problem is usually formulated as a set partitioning or a set covering problem. The objective of the set partitioning problem is to find a cost minimal subset of duties that covers each task exactly once. Each duty can only be full or no part of the solution. Contrary, the set covering formulation guarantees that each task is covered at least once.

The set partitioning problem is defined as follows: Let I be the set of all tasks to be covered and J the set of all feasible duties. A cost c_j is associated with each duty $j \in J$ and for the decision variables a_{ij} and x_j the following holds:

$$a_{ij} = \begin{cases} 1, & \text{if task } i \in I \text{ is part of duty } j \in J \\ 0, & \text{else,} \end{cases}$$

$$x_j = \begin{cases} 1, & \text{if duty } j \in J \text{ is part of the solution} \\ 0, & \text{else.} \end{cases}$$

The mathematical program can be written as:

$$\min \quad \sum_{j \in J} c_j x_j \tag{3.1}$$

$$s.t. \quad \sum_{j \in J} a_{ij} x_j = 1 \qquad \forall i \in I \tag{3.2}$$

$$x_j \in \{0,1\} \qquad \forall j \in J. \tag{3.3}$$

The objective is to minimize cost (Equation (3.1)). Equations (3.2) guarantee that each task is covered exactly once. Constraints (3.3) state that x_j are binary decision variables.

By replacing the equality signs " = " in the Constraints (3.2) by inequality signs " ≥ ", the formulation of the master problem as a set covering problem is obtained:

$$\min \quad \sum_{j \in J} c_j x_j \tag{3.4}$$

$$s.t. \quad \sum_{j \in J} a_{ij} x_j \geq 1 \qquad \forall i \in I \tag{3.5}$$

$$x_j \in \{0,1\} \qquad \forall j \in J. \tag{3.6}$$

Equations (3.5) guarantee that each task is covered at least once and not exactly once as it is in the set partitioning problem.

In many applications, the number of feasible duties is high. Therefore, the complete enumeration of both formulations can be inefficiently. Hoffman and Padberg (2009) note, that both problems are NP-hard. Additionally, for large-scale problem instances, the set partitioning formulation might lead to high computational effort due to the strong restriction of Constraints (3.2). By introducing a penalty cost factor c_{over} for covering a task more than once, the problem can be reformulated as a set covering problem (Albers (2009)). Let n_{over} denote the number of service deliveries that are covered more than once. Then, the set covering formulation is as follows:

$$\min \quad \sum_{j\in J} c_j x_j + c_{over} n_{over} \tag{3.7}$$

$$s.t. \quad \sum_{j\in J} a_{ij} x_j \geq 1 \qquad \forall i \in I \tag{3.8}$$

$$\sum_{j\in J}\sum_{i\in I} a_{ij} x_j - n_{over} \leq |I| \tag{3.9}$$

$$x_j \in \{0,1\} \qquad \forall j \in J \tag{3.10}$$

$$n_{over} \geq 0. \tag{3.11}$$

The objective is to find a crew schedule at minimum cost considering penalty cost for covering tasks more than once (Equation (3.7)). Constraints (3.8) ensure that a service delivery is covered at least once. Constraints (3.9) limit n_{over}. The solution of the set covering formulation (3.7) - (3.10) leads to less computational effort than the solution of the set partitioning formulation (3.1) - (3.3).

3.2.2 Subproblem

The master problem examines a given set of feasible duties. The duties are generated by the subproblem. Early approaches to generate duties are based on local improvement heuristics (Gershkoff (1989), Anbil et al. (1991)). But in the last decades, the approaches for the duty generation utilize more and more structural characteristics of the underlying problem and generate duties by network models (Lavoie et al. (1988), Barnhart et al. (1994), Vance et al. (1997)). In this thesis, the subproblem of the crew scheduling problem is based on network models. Therefore, we review different models in Section 3.2.2.1. In Section 3.2.2.2, approaches for the network representation are demonstrated.

3.2.2.1 Network Models

The subproblem can be formulated as a network flow problem based on a directed graph. The objective of a network flow algorithm is to transfer a given quantity of goods through a network at minimum cost (Goldberg et al. (1990)). The network consists of nodes that are connected by directed arcs. In general, the nodes are associated with cost and capacities.

Minimum Cost Flow Problem The basic model is the minimum cost flow problem (MCFP). We are given a graph $G(V,A)$ with node set V and arc set A. The flow from node $i \in V$ to node $j \in V$ is given by x_{ij}. Each arc $(i,j) \in A$ is associated with cost c_{ij}, a lower (B_{ij}^{lower}) and an upper (B_{ij}^{upper}) bound representing the capacity constraints. The demand and supply for each node $i \in V$ is denoted by β_i. $\beta_i > 0$ represents a supply and $\beta_i < 0$ a demand, respectively. The mathematical formulation of the MCFP is as follows (Glover et al. (1974)):

$$\min \quad \sum_{(i,j)\in A} c_{ij} x_{ij} \tag{3.12}$$

$$s.t. \quad \sum_{(i,j)\in A} x_{ij} - \sum_{(j,i)\in A} x_{ji} = \beta_i \qquad \forall i \in V \tag{3.13}$$

$$B_{ij}^{lower} \leq x_{ij} \leq B_{ij}^{upper} \qquad \forall (i,j) \in A. \tag{3.14}$$

The objective (3.12) of the MCFP is to minimize the total cost. Equations (3.13) ensure the flow conservation, i.e., the satisfaction of all demands by in- and outgoing arcs. Constraints (3.14) state that all the capacity constraints are respected.

Shortest Path Problem The shortest path problem (SPP) is a special case of the MCFP. In this problem, the shortest or cost minimal path from a source or origin o to a sink or destination d is determined. In contrast to the MCFP, the flow x_{ij} is a value between 0 and 1 to avoid circles with negative cost. Additionally, the source node o has a supply of $\beta_o = 1$ and the sink node d a demand of $\beta_d = -1$, all other nodes $i \in V \backslash \{o,d\}$ have no demands or supply, i.e., $\beta_i = 0$. The mathematical formulation of the SPP is as follows (Desrosiers et al. (1995)):

$$\min \quad \sum_{(i,j)\in A} c_{ij} x_{ij} \tag{3.15}$$

$$s.t. \quad \sum_{(i,j)\in A} x_{ij} - \sum_{(j,i)\in A} x_{ji} = \begin{cases} 1, & \text{for } i = o \\ 0, & \forall i \in V \setminus \{o,d\} \\ -1, & \text{for } i = d \end{cases} \tag{3.16}$$

$$0 \leq x_{ij} \leq 1 \qquad \forall (i,j) \in A. \tag{3.17}$$

Shortest Path Problem with Resource Constraints Since the subproblem has to consider multiple constraints in the process of generating feasible duties, the SPP is not sufficient in many applications. By defining the constraints as limits for feasible resource consumptions of a path, the subproblem can be formulated as a shortest path problem with resource constraints (SPPRC). Multiple survey review deals with the SPPRC. To get a more detailed overview of the SPPRC and of the general graph theory, we refer the interested reader to Desaulniers et al. (1998a), Irnich and Desaulniers (2005), and Cormen et al. (1990). In the following, we will describe the SPPRC based on the approach of Desrosiers et al. (1995).

Consider a directed acyclic graph $G(V,A)$ with a given set of nodes $V = N \cup \{o,d\}$ and arcs A. N is the set of nodes that can be visited by a path p with origin o and destination d. A sequence of nodes $i_0, i_1, \ldots, i_Z$ is defined as path p in G. All paths start at the origin $i_0 = o$ and end at the destination $i_Z = d$. Each node is connected to the subsequent node by an arc $(i_{z-1}, i_z) \in A$ $(1 \leq z \leq Z)$. Each arc $(i,j) \in A$ is associated with cost c_{ij}. Hence, the cost of a path p is the sum of the cost of the corresponding arcs, i.e., $c_p = \sum_{z=1}^{Z} c_{i_{z-1} i_z}$. Since a directed acyclic graph is given, each node is visited at most once.

Let R be the set of resources that represent the constraints of the underlying problem. Each arc $(i,j) \in A$ is associated with a resource consumption of t_{ij}^r for the corresponding resource $r \in R$. For each node $i \in V$ and each resource $r \in R$, the resource constraints intervals $\left[a_i^r, b_i^r\right]$ are given. The intervals restrict the amounts of resources used by the path that starts at the origin o and ends at the destination d. The consumptions of the different resources $r \in R$ are cumulated along the path. Let T_i^r be the accumulated consumption of resource $r \in R$ for a path from the origin o to node $i \in V$. A path that arrives at node $i \in V$ with a usage rate less than a_i^r units of resource $r \in R$ becomes feasible by expanding the path until a_i^r is reached, i.e., wasting resource r until a_i^r is reached. But, a path that arrives at $i \in V$ with a usage greater than b_i^r is infeasible. Only arcs $(i,j) \in A$ with $a_i^r + t_{ij}^r \leq b_j^r$ $(r \in R)$ are considered.

The definition of the SPPRC is as follows: The objective is to find a feasible path p from origin o to destination d at minimum cost, i.e., a sequence of nodes $i_o, i_1, \dots, i_Z$ and associated resource consumption $T_{i_z}^r, 0 \leq z \leq Z$, for all $r \in R$ such that:

1. $(i_{z-1}, i_z) \in A$, for $1 \leq z \leq Z$, with $i_0 = o$ and $i_Z = d$;
2. $T_{i_{z-1}}^r + t_{i_{z-1},i_z}^r \leq T_{i_z}^r, 1 \leq z \leq Z$ and $r \in R$;
3. the resource interval constraints are fulfilled at each node, i.e., $a_{i_z}^r \leq T_{i_z}^r \leq b_{i_z}^r, 0 \leq z \leq Z$ and $r \in R$;
4. the total cost c_p of path p is minimal among all feasible paths.

We denote the flow variables by $x_{ij}, (i,j) \in A$ and the resource variables by $T_i^r, i \in V$, $r \in R$. The mathematical formulation of the SPPRC is as follows:

$$\min \quad \sum_{(i,j)\in A} c_{ij} x_{ij} \tag{3.18}$$

$$\text{s.t.} \quad \sum_{j\in V} x_{ij} - \sum_{j\in V} x_{ji} = \begin{cases} 1, & \text{for } i = o \\ 0, & \forall i \in N \\ -1, & \text{for } i = d \end{cases} \tag{3.19}$$

$$x_{ij} \geq 0 \qquad \forall (i,j) \in A \tag{3.20}$$

$$x_{ij}(T_i^r + t_{ij}^r - T_j^r) \geq 0 \qquad \forall (i,j) \in A, \forall r \in R \tag{3.21}$$

$$a_i^r \leq T_i^r \leq b_i^r \qquad \forall i \in V, \forall r \in R. \tag{3.22}$$

3.2.2.2 Network Representation

As mentioned above, the use of the presented network models requires an appropriate network representation. For the crew scheduling problem, different network representations are possible to generate feasible duties. This section reviews the approaches.

To represent all possible tasks or activities in a network, two general options are possible: an *activity-on-arc* representation and an *activity-on-node* representation. The activity-on-arc representation models tasks on arcs, the activity-on-node representation on nodes respectively (Kolisch et al. (1995)). Figures 3.1 and 3.2 show an example of tasks a, b, c, d. Task a is followed by task b. However, task b is the predecessor of task c or d. In Figure 3.1, the tasks are represented by arcs and results in an event orientated representation. Contrary, Figure 3.2 represents the tasks by nodes and the diagram shows a task orientated representation.

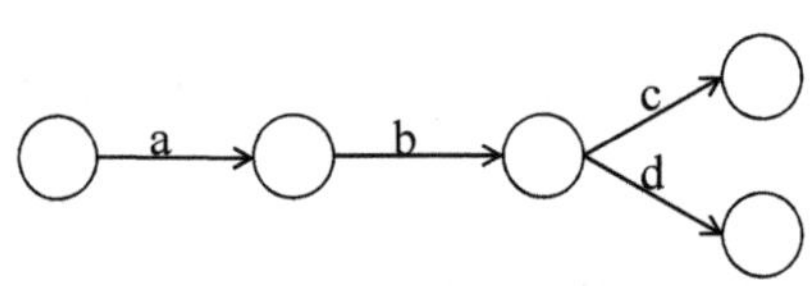

Figure 3.1: Activity-on-Arc Representation

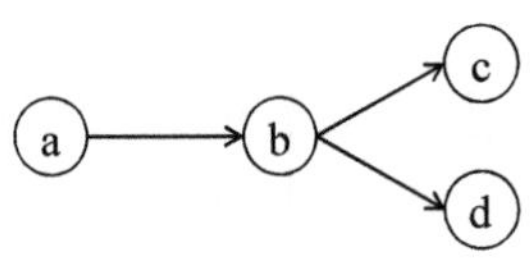

Figure 3.2: Activity-on-Node Representation

To consider paths in a network, the time and space have to be included in the network representation. Two different networks can be distinguished: a *time-line network* and a *connection network*. The time-line network is based on activity-on-arc representation and the connection network uses activity-on-node representation. Comparisons of the different approaches can be found in Barnhart et al. (1994) (for a long-haul airline crew scheduling problem), Desaulniers et al. (1999) (for a regional airline crew scheduling problem), Engineer et al. (2008), and Steinzen et al. (2010).

In a time-line network, the starting and ending point of a task are represented by nodes. To represent a task, the departure nodes and the corresponding arrival nodes are connected by an arc. The time-line network cannot explicitly exclude an infeasible connection.

In contrast to the time-line network, the tasks are represented by nodes in the connection network. The feasible connections between different tasks are modeled by arcs. An arc is a transition in time and space.

Figure 3.3 shows the example of a connection network with 5 tasks and 4 locations. The x-axis represents the time and the different locations are displayed on the y-axis.

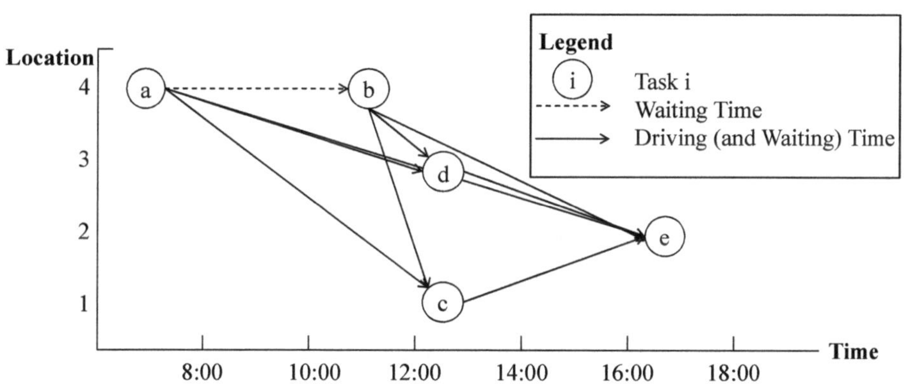

Figure 3.3: Connection Network

The nodes represent the location and the time where the corresponding task has to start. Directed arcs are generated between two nodes and represent feasible connections from one task to another. The arcs between two nodes indicate driving and/or waiting times, depending on the need of changing the location or not. In Figure 3.3, there is no arc between tasks c and d, because it is not possible to drive from task c to d before the start of task d, i.e., the connection is not feasible.

3.3 Solution Approaches

In Section 3.2, the crew scheduling problem was decomposed into a master problem and a subproblem. In this section, the interaction of the master problem with the subproblem and the corresponding solution approaches are described. Since the number of possible routes J may be large, the explicit search can be computationally expensive. Therefore, we consider a reasonable subset J' and solve a LP-relaxation of the master problem which leads to the restricted master problem (RMP). The RMP is solved by the simplex method. If duties with negative reduced cost are found in the subproblem, the corresponding columns are added to the RMP and the RMP is re-optimized. We iterate between solving the subproblem and re-optimizing the master problem until no more negative reduced cost columns are found. To obtain the optimal integer solution, we apply branch-and-price.

First, we solve a linear problem by column generation and the decomposition principle for linear programs (Section 3.3.1). In a next step, an integer problem is defined (Section 3.3.2). To generate integer solutions, column generation is embedded in a branch-and-bound tree, referred to as branch-and-price. Finally, it is shown how the subproblem searches for new feasible duties within the column generation process (Section 3.3.3).

3.3.1 Decomposition for Linear Programs and Column Generation

The crew scheduling problem is a large-scale optimization problem. The Dantzig-Wolfe decomposition (Dantzig and Wolfe (1960)) and column generation are often used to solve this kind of large-scale integer programming problems. The decomposition approach adresses the linking structure of the crew scheduling problem at a superior, coordinating level, but the subsystems are addressed at a subordinated level to exploit any special structure at the algorithmic level (Lübbecke and Desrosiers

(2005)). We follow the approach of Lübbecke and Desrosiers (2005) to present the decomposition principle in linear programs.

The following linear program is typically called the *master problem* (MP):

$$\min \quad \sum_{j \in J} c_j x_j \tag{3.23}$$

$$s.t. \quad \sum_{j \in J} a_j x_j \geq b \tag{3.24}$$

$$x_j \geq 0, \forall j \in J. \tag{3.25}$$

The MP can be solved by the simplex method (Dantzig and Wolfe (1960)). The simplex method searches in each iteration for a non-basic variable to price out and enter the basis, referred to as *pricing step*. Let π be the non-negative vector of dual variables that corresponds to the Inequality (3.24) of the MP. Then, the pricing step searches for

$$\arg\min\{\bar{c_j} = c_j - \pi^T a_j | j \in J\}. \tag{3.26}$$

In case of a large $|J|$, the complexity of the pricing step is high. To reduce computational time, only a subset $J' \subseteq J$ is considered. This leads to the RMP:

$$\min \quad \sum_{j \in J'} c_j x_j \tag{3.27}$$

$$s.t. \quad \sum_{j \in J'} a_j x_j \geq b \tag{3.28}$$

$$x_j \geq 0, \forall j \in J'. \tag{3.29}$$

The simplex method provides the dual variables of the RMP. After optimization, the dual values of the non-basic variables are positive and those of the basic variables are equal to 0. In the following, the dual variable of the optimal solution $\bar{x}$ of the RMP is denoted by $\bar{\pi}$. In J', columns with negative reduced cost do not exist, but there might be one within the set of all columns $SC = \{a_j | j \in J\}$. The pricing step includes the search for new columns with negative reduced cost that are given implicitly. For columns a_j with corresponding cost coefficients c_j the subproblem is defined as follows:

$$\bar{c}^* := \min\{c_j - \bar{\pi}^T a_j | a_j \in SC\}. \tag{3.30}$$

The best found column a^* is given by:

$$a^* := \arg\min\{c_j - \bar{\pi}^T a_j | a_j \in SC\}. \tag{3.31}$$

The subproblem searches for columns that can improve the current solution of the RMP. For $\bar{c}^* \geq 0$, $\bar{x}$ is optimal for the MP. If $\bar{c}^*$ is negative, a^* is a new column that can improve the current optimal solution. The RMP is enlarged by the new column and the RMP is re-optimized. Solving the column generation subproblem and the re-optimization of the RMP is repeated until no more columns with negative reduced cost are found. This process is called *(delayed) column generation.* Figure 3.4 presents a systematic outline.

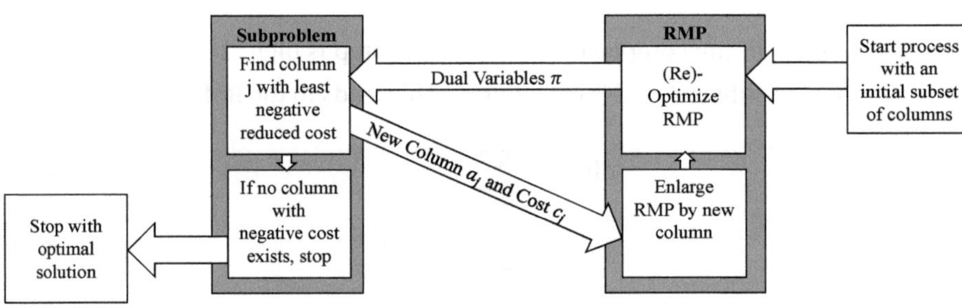

Figure 3.4: Outline of Column Generation Process

The optimal solution $\bar{z}$ provides an upper bound for the optimal solution z^* of the MP. For each solution of the RMP, a $\bar{\kappa} \geq \sum_{j \in j} x_j$ exists, that allows to determine a lower bound for the optimal solution of the MP, i.e., the optimal solution z^* cannot decrease more than $\bar{\kappa}\bar{c}^*$ (Lasdon (2002)):

$$\bar{z} + \bar{\kappa}\bar{c}^* \leq z^* \leq \bar{z}. \tag{3.32}$$

Using the bounds, the solution quality can be verified at any time during the run of a column generation algorithm to enforce, for instance, a termination of the process after the realization of a certain quality. Other possibilities to determine bounds are given for instance by Farley (1990) and Vanderbeck (1996).

3.3.2 Integer Crew Scheduling Optimization

The previous section described the non-integral solution of a linear program by column generation. In the following, column generation is embedded in a branch-and bound tree to generate integer solutions, referred to as branch-and-price.

The integer program is referred to as *integer master problem* (MP_{IP}):

$$\min \quad \sum_{j \in J} c_j x_j \tag{3.33}$$

$$s.t. \quad \sum_{j \in J} a_j x_j \geq b \tag{3.34}$$

$$x_j \in \mathbb{N}_0, \forall j \in J. \tag{3.35}$$

The basic idea of integer column generation is to solve the MP_{IP} not directly, but to solve a linear programming relaxation of the RMP (3.27) - (3.29). The solution of the RMP is in most cases a non-integral solution. Then, at every node of the branch-and-bound tree, column generation is performed. Branching is applied when no columns with negative reduced cost are found in the subproblem and the solution of the linear program does not satisfy the integrality conditions. Branching is repeated until the optimal integral solution is found.

The branching schemes are specific for the corresponding problem. The better the lower bounds and the solutions resulting from branching, the faster the optimal integral solution can be found. That is why a good branching scheme should be based on those rules that can lead to good lower bounds quickly. General branching schemes are provided by Vanderbeck (2000) or Achterberg (2005). Linderoth and Savelsbergh (1999) provide various branch-and-bound strategies. A general branching scheme for the crew scheduling problem can be found in Foster and Ryan (1981). The branching scheme of Foster and Ryan (1981) will be discussed in detail for the specific service routing problem in Section 6.1.1.2.

According to Vanderbeck (1996), in many applications a difficulty with column generation is the *tailing-off-effect*, i.e., the large number of iterations needed to prove the optimality of the solution of the linear program. The effect is a potential issue at every node of the search tree. Besides that, the pricing step can lead to high computational time. Especially the search for the optimal solution of an integer program can be very time consuming. Therefore, several heuristics can be applied to find a near-optimal solution within acceptable computational time.

The main heuristics can be divided into two heuristic branch-and-price approaches: The first approach is very common for complicated subproblems (Albers (2009)). If the computational time for solving the subproblem is much higher than the time to solve the RMP, columns are only generated at the root node.

The second approach is referred to as *variable fixing* and is common for very large-scale problems. The general idea is to branch by fixing variables $x_j = 0$, such that the branch-and-bound tree is partially explored depth-first. At each node new columns are generated to retrieve the solution quality which is lost due to fixing heuristics (Grönkvist (2005)). Albers (2009) used a SCORE-system to decide on the variables to be fixed. A good SCORE-system is important to get a good solution quality. For each variable, a SCORE is determined. Based on the SCORE-value the variables can be chosen based of one of the following approaches:

1. All fractional variables with a SCORE-value greater than a predetermined value τ are fixed.

2. If the number of variables with a SCORE-value greater than τ is lower than a predetermined value pv, other fractional variables are fixed to get pv variables that are set equal to 1.

3. Alternatively to a predetermined number pv, the rounded value of a fraction fr of the sum of all fractional variable values is applied.

Although variable fixing leads in most cases only to an approximation of the optimal solution, it may provide a helpful initial upper bound for the branch-and-price algorithm.

3.3.3 Generation of Duties in Subproblem

The subproblem is part of the iterative column generation process and generates duties that can improve the current solution of the RMP. The subproblem is represented by a connection network and modeled as a SPPRC (Desrosiers et al. (1995)) to find new columns with negative reduced cost. The columns with negative reduced cost are added to the RMP and the RMP is resolved. If the subproblem cannot identify columns with negative reduced cost, the LP-relaxation of the master problem is optimal. The SPPRC can be solved by dynamic programming (Bellman (1957)). The approach is enhanced by a *label-pulling* algorithm or a *label-reaching* algorithm.

A label (T_i^R, C_i) at a node i represents the status of the reduced cost C_i, which is a function of the state and the quantity of each resource $\left(T_i^1, T_i^2, ..., T_i^{|R|}\right)$ used by a feasible path P_i. P_i denotes the path from the source node o to node i. Starting with an initial label at the source node, new labels at nodes that are reachable via adjacent arcs are created. A label is only saved if the corresponding path is feasible. After the successive extensions of the path represented by labels, the labels are saved at the sink node. The labels at the sink node represent complete paths. The path with the minimum cost is the optimal solution of the subproblem. The generation of all feasible paths is a complete enumeration. This can lead to complex procedures and can be very time consuming. To avoid this, dominance and efficiency are considered during the generation of paths (Albers (2009)). A label (T_i^{1R}, C_i^1) is *dominated* by a label (T_i^{2R}, C_i^2) at node i, i.e., $(T_i^{1R}, C_i^1) < (T_i^{2R}, C_i^2)$, if and only if $T_1^R \leq T_2^R$ and $C_1 < C_2$ or $T_1^R < T_2^R$ and $C_1 \leq C_2$ for all $r \in R$. A label (T_i^R, C_i) which is not dominated by another label at node i is called *efficient*. The corresponding path P_i is also called efficient.

The label-pulling algorithm creates labels in an efficient way to solve the SPPRC by a dynamic programming algorithm which ignores dominated labels (Desrochers and Soumis (1988)). The label-pulling algorithm "pulls" all labels to be saved for the corresponding node, i.e., the labels of a node j are created by extending feasible labels (T_i^R, C_i) of its predecessors based on the connecting arcs $(i,j) \in A$. If the resource conditions are respected, i.e., $T_i^r + t_{ij}^r \leq b_j^r$ for $r \in R$, a new feasible label (T_j^R, C_j) with $C_j = C_i + c_{ij}$ and $T_j^R = \max\left\{a_j^r, T_i^r + t_{ij}^r | r \in R\right\}$ at node j is found. All labels which are saved at the sink node represent feasible solutions of the SPPRC. The one with the least cost represents the optimal solution of the SPPRC.

Besides the label-pulling algorithm a second possibility to create labels is the label-reaching algorithm. It extends labels to several successors. This leads to a higher memory management compared to the label-pulling process. However, it is possible to terminate the label-reaching process after the generation of one label with negative reduced cost at the sink node. Desrosiers et al. (1995) develops an algorithm to solve the SPPRC by dynamic programming. To avoid extensive feasibility tests during the label process, a *K-th shortest path problem* (K-SPP) is solved instead of the SPPRC. The K-SPP is a generalized version of the SPP (Equations (3.15)-(3.17)). In the K-SPP, the resource constraints are ignored during the generation of paths. Instead, the K shortest paths $\{P_1, P_2, ..., P_K\}$ are generated and sorted by their corresponding cost in increasing order $(c(P_1) \leq c(P_2) \leq ... \leq c(P_K))$. It is important that there exists no path P_i with $c(P_i) < c(P_K)$ for all $i \neq 1, ..., K$. In a next step the feasibility of the paths is tested. The feasibility test starts with the shortest path P_1. If the path P_1 is not feasible, the second shortest path P_2 is considered. The feasibility test terminates after the first feasible path has been found. The corresponding path is the least cost feasible path and represents the same solution as the optimal solution of the SPPRC.

For an extensive overview about label algorithms to find the K shortest paths in a network model, we refer to Ahuja et al. (1993). It is obvious that for small K solving the K-SPP is less time consuming than solving a SPPRC. However, for large K it leads to a high number of labels. Therefore, the trade-off between memory management and the complexity of feasibility tests has to be considered, where an appropriate combination of both approaches may be useful.

4 Local and Global Search Heuristics

Besides the scheduling of personnel, the exploration of different delivery plans is a second challenge of this thesis. According to Chapter 2, common methods to explore different neighborhood solutions are local random search, steepest descent, simulated annealing, and tabu search approaches. Local random search and steepest descent are applied until no more improvements of the objective function value can be found. The best solution found is the local optimum. Since the local optimum is often not the optimal solution, global search heuristics are applied to escape from the local optimum. In this chapter, we will generally illustrate the different approaches based on minimization problems.

Section 4.1 gives a detailed description of approaches to find a local optimum. Local random search is introduced in Section 4.1.1. Section 4.1.2 deals with steepest descent approaches. Section 4.2 shows how to escape from a local optimum by the help of simulated annealing (Section 4.2.1) and tabu search (Section 4.2.2).

4.1 Local Search Heuristics

Local search heuristics explore different solution spaces and terminate if no more improvements can be found. This thesis focuses on the two common approaches. Section 4.1.1 illustrates the local random search approach and Section 4.1.2 describes the steepest descent approach.

4.1.1 Local Random Search

The local random search approach is based on a combinatorial optimization problem (Voudouris (1999)). The problem is defined by (Λ, f), where Λ represents the set of all feasible solutions and f is the objective function of the problem. The objective is to

N. Holtvogt, *The Service Routing Problem*, Edition KWV,
https://doi.org/10.1007/978-3-658-24126-1_4

find $g^* \in \Lambda$, so that $f(g^*)$ is minimized, i.e., $f(g^*) = \min_{g \in \Lambda} f(g)$. $N(g)$ is referred to the neighborhood of a feasible solution $g \in \Lambda$. The neighborhood $N(g)$ consists of all solutions that can be achieved from g in a single step. A step refers to the use of an operator that transforms g to $g' \in \Lambda, g' \neq g$, by a marginal modification of g. A local minimum g of f is found if there exists no other $g' \in N(g)$ with a lower objective function value, i.e.,

$$f(g') \geq f(g), \forall g' \in \Lambda. \tag{4.1}$$

After starting with an initial solution, the algorithm terminates after no more improvements can be found, i.e., the *local minimum* is found. There exists multiple ways to decide on the next possible solution g' that improves the current solution. The characteristic of local random search is to explore the neighborhood in a random order and to accept the first feasible solution that has a lower objective function value than the current solution.

Figure 4.1 illustrates the steps of the local random search approach. The process starts with an initial solution g. Then, a random solution $g' \in N(g)$ is chosen and g' is no longer an element of $N(g)$. The corresponding objective function value $f(g')$ is compared to the objective function value of the current solution $f(g)$. If $f(g') < f(g)$, then the solution is accepted. If $f(g') \geq f(g)$, then the solution is not accepted. In both cases, a new random solution is chosen. However, for $f(g') < f(g)$ the current solution g is set to g' and the neighborhood of the new solution is determined. The process terminates when the set $N(g)$ is empty. The current best solution is the solution of the algorithm.

The computational time to find a local optimum by local random search depends highly on the size of the neighborhood (Voudouris (1999)). The local optimum does not necessarily represent the global optimum of the problem. One method for local random search to find solutions with a lower objective function value is the repetition of the algorithm in a different random order of the neighborhood search. This process can be repeated multiple times until a predetermined number of runs has been performed. The best solution of all runs is then chosen.

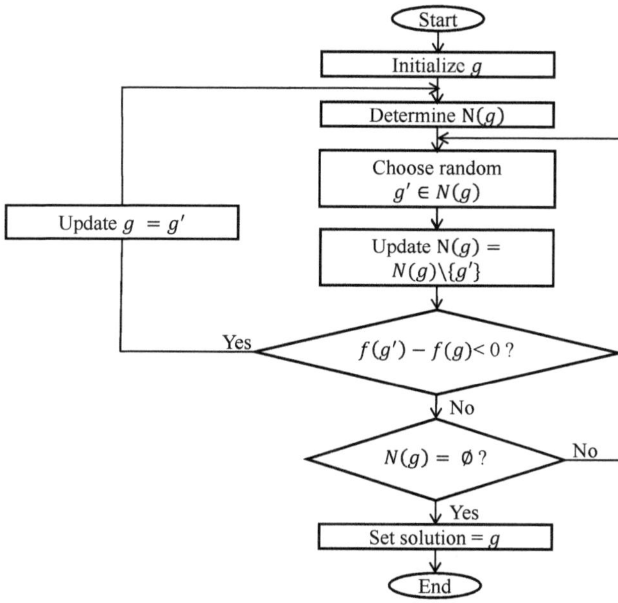

Figure 4.1: Process of Local Random Search

4.1.2 Steepest Descent

Steepest descent explores the entire neighborhood $N(g)$ of a solution $g \in \Lambda$ and accepts the neighbor solution g' with the smallest objective function value, i.e., $g' = \arg\min_{\tilde{g} \in N(g)} f(\tilde{g})$. Cauchy (1847) introduced the general idea of the steepest descent approach by using the gradient to solve the equation $f(g) = 0$. It is assumed that f is a non-negative and continuous function. Figure 4.2 illustrates the general process of the steepest descent approach. After the determination of an initial solution $g \in \Lambda$, g' with $g' = \arg\min_{\tilde{g} \in N(g)} f(\tilde{g})$ is determined. If $f(g') < f(g)$, the new solution is accepted and the current solution g is set to g'. The neighborhood of the new solution g is determined and again the solution with the smallest objective function value within the entire neighborhood is searched. If $f(g') \geq f(g)$, the algorithm terminates and the current solution g is the local optimum of the underlying problem.

Steepest descent is based on the fact that a continuous function decreases by tak-

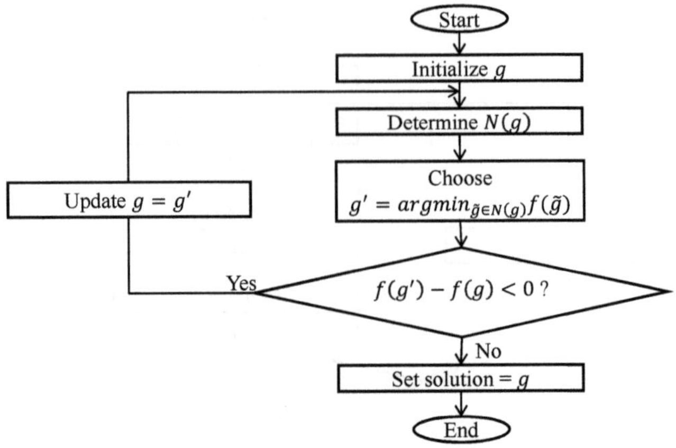

Figure 4.2: Process of Steepest Descent

ing a step along the direction of the negative gradient of f (Meza (2010)). To find the minimum of $f(g)$, $g \in \mathbb{R}^n$, we have to take the gradient $\nabla f(g)$ of f. The search direction is given by $-\nabla f(g)$. Along the search direction a step is computed by

$$g_{i+1} = g_i - sl_i \nabla f(g), i \geq 0. \tag{4.2}$$

sl_i is referred to as step length and can be a fix number or can be changed in every iteration. It follows that $f(g_0) \geq f(g_1) \geq ...$, so that the minimum can be found through multiple iterations (Wang (2008)).

Figure 4.3 illustrates how the steepest descent approach finds a minimum (Wang (2008)). The process starts with an initial value g_0 and takes steps along the direction of the negative gradient with the fastest change. The process terminates at the minimum in this example. The steepest descent approach is a very common approach due to its conceptual simplicity to determine an existing (local) minimum. However, special cases can require high computational time (Avriel (2003)).

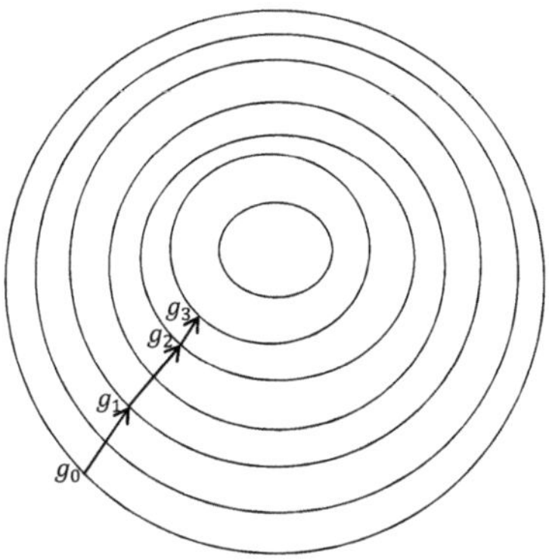

Figure 4.3: General Idea of Steepest Descent

4.2 Global Search Heuristics

Local random search and steepest descent can help to find a good feasible solution, but the optimality of the solution is not guaranteed (Joubert (2007)). It is not known how close the local optimum is to the solution with the best objective function value, the *global optimum*.

Figure 4.4 illustrates the general idea of global search heuristics based on a minimization problem with a continuous objective function $f(g)$. If a local search heuris-

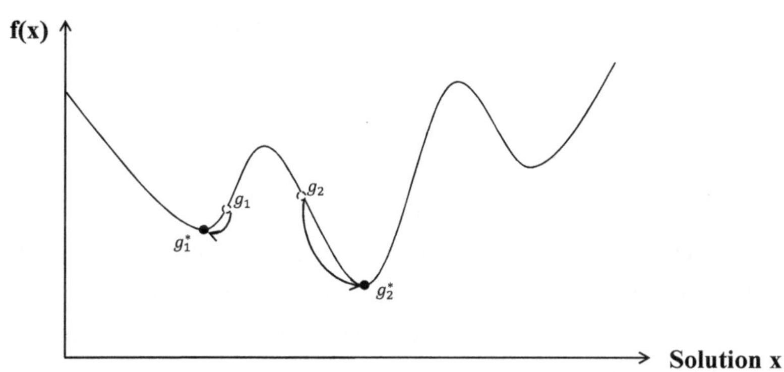

Figure 4.4: Influence of Initial Solution on Solution Quality

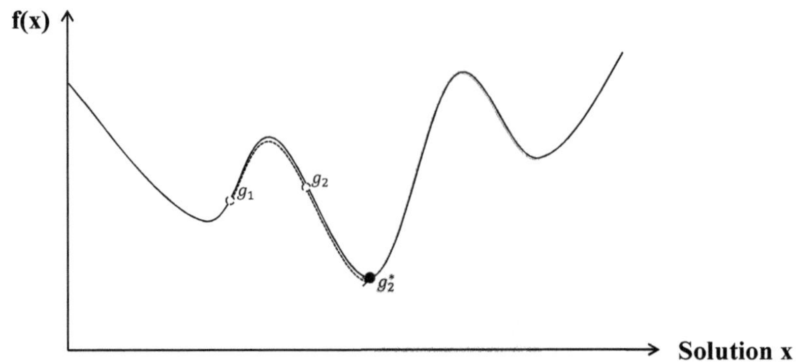

Figure 4.5: Influence of Global Search Heuristics on Solution Quality

tic starts with an initial solution in g_1, it results in the local optimum g_1^*. However, the same search heuristic can lead to the local optimum g_2^* with the initial solution g_2, which is the global optimum.

Figure 4.5 illustrates the use of a global search heuristic for an example. The heuristics allow solutions that worsen the objective function value. With the initial solution g_1, the solution reaches the solution g_2 by accepting a higher objective function value, the solution moves along the dotted line before reaching the optimal solution g_2^* for this example.

In the following, two global search heuristics are described which allow for instance the possibility to perform a change from g_1 to g_2: simulated annealing (Section 4.2.1) and tabu search (Section 4.2.2).

4.2.1 Simulated Annealing

Simulated annealing is a global search heuristic and was introduced by Kirkpatrick et al. (1983) and Cerný (1985). The approach is a generalization of the iterative improvement approach to combinatorial optimization problems and is similar to the algorithm for the annealing of solids (van Laarhoven et al. (1992)). The basic idea of simulated annealing is to accept occasionally solutions that worsen the objective

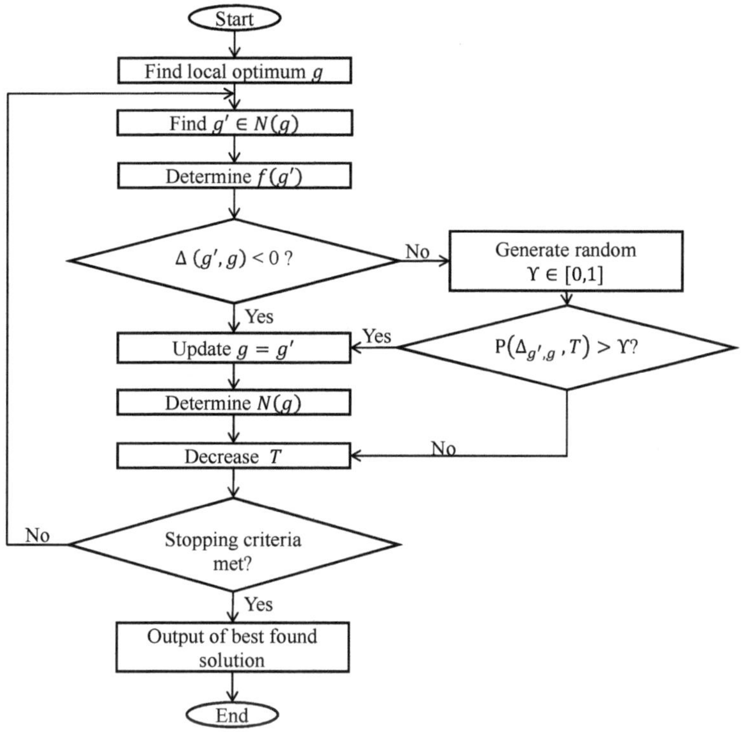

Figure 4.6: Process of Simulated Annealing

function value with a certain acceptance probability. The acceptance probability is determined following the Boltzmann probability factor (Kirkpatrick et al. (1983)).

The function for the acceptance probability is denoted by $P(\Delta_{g',g}, T) = \exp^{-\frac{\Delta_{g',g}}{T}}$. The difference $\Delta_{g',g} = f(g') - f(g)$ indicates the change in the objective function value by exchanging element g by g'. $\Delta_{g',g}$ is divided by temperature T, i.e., the probability to accept a worse solution is exponentially decreasing in temperature. Figure 4.6 shows a flowchart of the algorithm we will apply in this thesis. Generally, the algorithm can start with any feasible solution. In this example, it starts with the local optimum g. Element g represents a specific assignment or setting that results in the locally minimal objective function value $f(g)$. Now another setting $g' \in N(g)$ is chosen randomly and the corresponding objective function value $f(g')$ is determined.

If $\Delta_{g',g} < 0$, the change from setting g to setting g' is accepted and g is set to g'. In a next step the temperature T is decreased. If a certain stopping criterion is met, e.g., a predetermined number of iterations is performed, then the process terminates and the solution of the algorithm is g. Otherwise a new $g' \in N(g)$ is chosen randomly and the process starts again.

If $\Delta_{g',g} \geq 0$, a random number $\Upsilon \in [0,1]$ is generated. If $P(\Delta_{g',g}, T) > \Upsilon$, then the solution is performed and T is decreased. Otherwise, the solution is denied and the temperature T is decreased. If a certain stopping criterion is met, the algorithm terminates with solution g. Otherwise, the process starts again.

One challenge of simulated annealing is to determine a good annealing schedule (Rutenbar (1989)). At the beginning of the algorithm, a starting temperature T_0 is required. The temperature is often determined by a problem specific heuristic. During the simulated annealing process the temperature can be decreased. A common method is the use of a cooling rate cr, i.e., after it iterations the temperature is set to $T_{it} = cr^{it} T_0$.

4.2.2 Tabu Search

Tabu search is a memory-based global search heuristic that was introduced by Glover (1986). The following description of the method is based on Sharda et al. (2006) and Joubert (2007). The idea of tabu search is the use of a *tabu list*, that contains recently examined solutions.

Figure 4.7 shows the flowchart of the approach. The algorithm can start with any feasible solution g with the objective function value $f(g)$. A feasible solution g' from the neighborhood $N(g)$ is chosen following a predetermined decision strategy. If there are no solutions within the neighborhood $N(g)$ that can improve the current objective function value, the solution g' with the lowest increase in the objective function value is chosen and g is set to g'. In a next step, the solution of the previous step is often chosen, because it leads to a decrease in the objective function value. To avoid these cyclic solutions, the previous solution is put on a tabu list. If there exists no feasible solution within the neighborhood $N(g)$ or a certain stopping criterion is

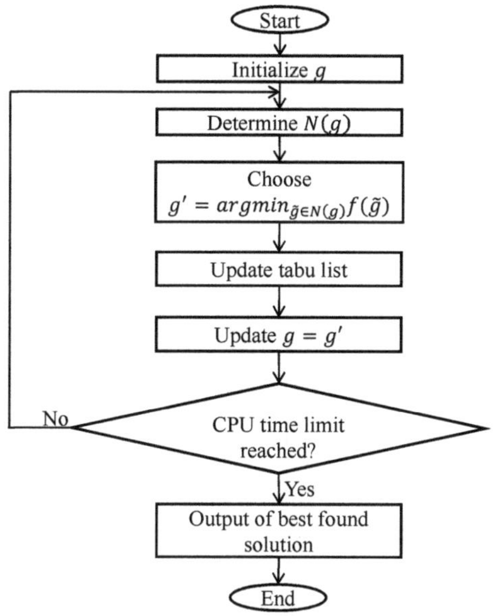

Figure 4.7: Process of Tabu Search

met, e.g., a given central processing unit (CPU) time limit, the algorithm terminates and the best solution found marks the solution of the approach. Else the current solution g is again set to the new solution g' and the process starts again.

The tabu list can be handled in different ways. Figure 4.8 illustrates that the management of the tabu list can be divided into two main approaches (Voß (2001), Domschke and Scholl (2010)): It is possible to use a static or a dynamic list.

A static list can either be strict or reactive. In a static and strict tabu list, a single element is put on the tabu list for a predetermined number of iterations. The choice of the number of iterations has a big influence on the solution quality of the tabu search approach (Scholl (1999)). In a static and reactive tabu list the number of iterations to block an element on the tabu list is based on the size and the type of the underlying problem (Scholl (1999)).

An example for a dynamic tabu list is the reverse elimination method (Domschke and Scholl (2010)). The reverse elimination method uses a running list that saves all

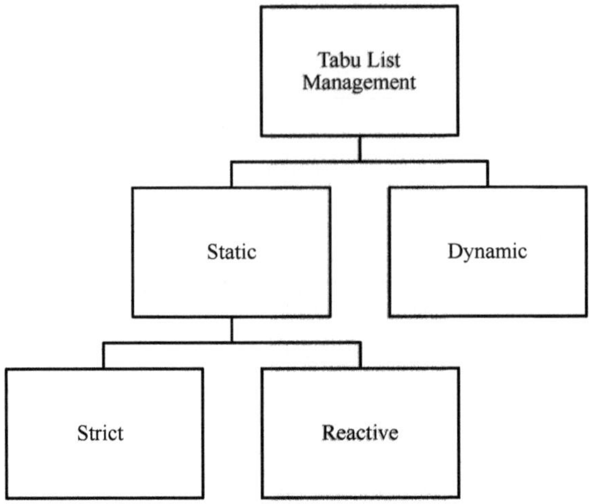

Figure 4.8: Classification of Tabu List Management

performed steps of the tabu search approach. For more details on dynamic tabu list management using the reverse elimination method can be found in Dammeyer and Voß (1993). The use of a constantly increasing running list leads to a high computational complexity. Approaches to minimize the size of the running list are for instance given by Voß (1996).

5 The Service Routing Problem

After providing the fundamental basis for this thesis, we focus on the service routing problem. The service routing problem combines crew scheduling and shifting of service times. The objective is to develop solution approaches to optimize both problems jointly. We model the problem and highlight the importance of shifting service times to decrease crew scheduling cost.

This chapter describes the general aspects of the service routing problem. Section 5.1 starts with the description of a possible application of the service routing problem to recall the general idea explained in Chapter 1. In Section 5.2, we focus on the problem specifications. Finally, Section 5.3 highlights the effect of shifting service times on crew scheduling cost to illustrate the importance of the service routing problem.

5.1 Exemplary Application

A possible application of the service routing problem is the maintenance of copy machines by "traveling repairmen" of a service company. We assume that the company has to maintain several copy machines at its customer's offices. Service has to be delivered at the latest after a predetermined usage rate. The usage data of the machines is given by the number of copies per time interval. For each customer-machine-combination, the starting times of the next required maintenance can be determined based on the current usage rate. However, all subsequent starting times of servicing a particular machine depend on the starting times of the previous maintenance of this machine - the later the starting time of the previous maintenance, the later are the limits of starting times of the following maintenances. The consideration of shifting of service times may influence the scheduling cost.

N. Holtvogt, *The Service Routing Problem*, Edition KWV,
https://doi.org/10.1007/978-3-658-24126-1_5

5.2 Problem Specifications

In this section, we report the problem specifications of the service routing problem. We start explaining the specific network structure and the characteristics of a service crew (Section 5.2.1). Then, we introduce relevant terms of the service routing problem in Sections 5.2.2 - 5.2.4. In Section 5.2.5, we specify the work time regulations based on German Law. Finally, we explain the cost structure of a service crew schedule in Section 5.2.6.

5.2.1 Network Structure and Service Crew

The network structure of the service routing problem is similar to the network structure of the classical vehicle routing problem (Section 2.2). We consider a homogeneous fleet of V *service crew members*. The service crew members are deployed to service M sites. The sites are geographically dispersed, so that the service crew members have to drive from site $i \in M$ to site $j \in M$ $(i \neq j)$ with a service vehicle. The traveling from one site to another site causes travel cost $c_{ij} \geq 0$ and travel time $t_{ij} \geq 0$. The service crew members are dispatched from a central depot, i.e., a service crew member starts the service duty at the depot by picking up the service vehicle and ends the duty by returning the vehicle to the depot.

In our application, one service crew member usually serves multiple sites during a duty and travels between sites. The material needed for the service delivery is in the service vehicle and/or at each site. The material is reused or negligible and therefore service vehicles can, for all practical purposes, service an unlimited number of sites. An arbitrary number of service crew members are scheduled to fulfill all required services. Since the number of available service crew members is unlimited, the daily number of service duties that can start at the depot is unrestricted.

5.2.2 Service Duty

The sequence of activities a service crew member has to perform is referred to as *service duty*. Figure 5.1 shows an example of a service duty.

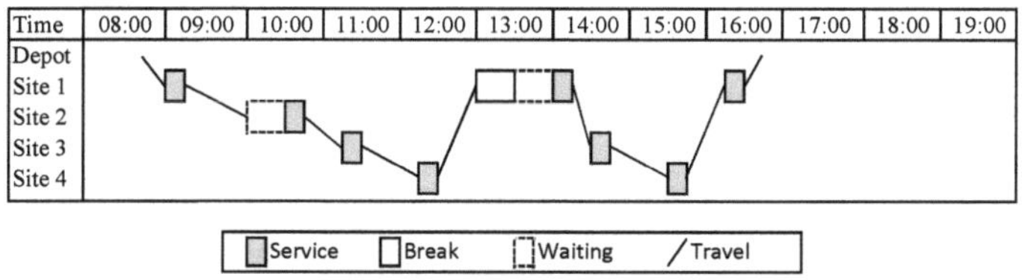

Figure 5.1: Service Duty

The example illustrates that a service duty always starts and ends at the depot. After the beginning of the service duty, the first activity in Figure 5.1 is the driving from the depot to site 1. At site 1 the next activity, service at site 1, is fulfilled. The service crew member's next activity is again driving, i.e., the service crew member has to drive to site 2. Before the service can be fulfilled, the service crew member has to wait in this example. Waiting is also an activity of a service duty. Next, a service delivery is performed followed by driving and servicing site 3 and 4. Then, after driving to site 1, the service crew member has a break followed by waiting and service activities. Three more service deliveries including the required driving from one site to another site are performed, before the service duty ends after returning to the depot.

In total, service duties consist of some or all of the following activities:

Service (delivery) describes the activity a service crew member has to fulfill at a certain site. The time it takes to service each site is denoted by sd and is referred to as *service delivery time.*

Driving is the activity of a service crew member to move from one site to another site. It is required to be able to deliver service at different sites. Travel time and travel cost occur.

Waiting describes the activity a service crew member performs when he or she is already at the site of the next service, but has to wait until the service delivery can be started. After a service delivery, a service crew member drives immediately to the site of the next service, so that possible waiting times occur only at the sites to be serviced next.

Breaks describe unpaid rest periods that are due to work time regulations. The specific work time regulations are described in Section 5.2.5.

To analyze service duties the durations, driving distances, work times, and break times are evaluated. Based on these values the cost of a schedule is determined.

5.2.3 Usage Rate and State of Site

The *usage rate* results from the demand that occurs at each site. The rate at a site m is denoted by d_m, i.e., in each time unit a deterministic and positive demand of d_m arises. We define the *state of site* m, X_m, as the number of demands that have been filled by site m since the last service. The maximum capacity of a site is denoted by D_m^{max}. We require that the state X_m does not exceed D_m^{max}. A service delivery leads to a reset of the state, i.e., $X_m = 0$. During a service delivery time sd, the demand of d_m still occurs and the state is set to zero immediately after the service. We denote the state of a site m at the beginning of the planning horizon by D_m^0, with $0 \leq D_m^0 \leq D_m^{max} - sd \cdot d_m$.

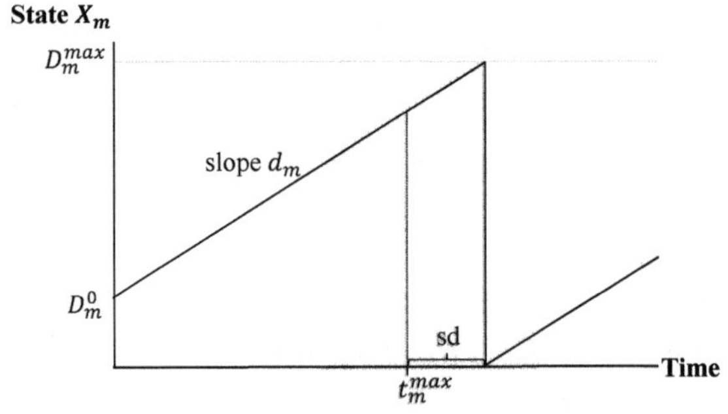

Figure 5.2: Development of State of Site m

Figure 5.2 illustrates the development of the state of site m. The state X_m is a linear function with slope d_m. The latest possible time to deliver service is denoted by t_m^{max} and is referred to as *latest service time*, i.e., if $t_m = t_m^{max} + sd$, then t_m is the point in time when the state of site m is equal to D_m^{max}. After the service, the state of X_m is reset to 0.

Based on the time t_m of the last service at site m, the latest service times t_m^{max} can be determined by the following equation:

$$t_m^{max} = t_m + \frac{D_m^{max}}{d_m} - sd. \tag{5.1}$$

Service can be delivered before the latest service time t_m^{max}, but it is not allowed to deliver service at any point of time after t_m^{max}.

5.2.4 Service Period and Service Table

The planning horizon to schedule the service crew members is based on days. Each site of the network has opening hours, i.e., demand at the sites occurs only during this time and service can only be provided during this time period. We use a discrete time model and divide the planning horizon into equal-length time periods. We set the length of the periods equal to the service time. The maximum distance between services at site m is $dis_m = \lfloor \frac{D_m^{max}}{d_m} - sd \rfloor$ periods.

A time period that includes a service delivery is called a *service period.* A time period without a service delivery is referred to as *non-service period.* The composition of service and non-service periods over all sites and time periods is referred to as *service table* ψ. A service table ψ is feasible, if the maximum distance between two service deliveries is not exceeded for any site. The set of all feasible service tables is denoted by Ψ.

Figure 5.3 shows the example of a service table. We assume that each site is open

	Day 1												Day 2			
Time Period	1	2	3	4	5	6	7	8	9	10	11	12	1	2	3	...
Site 1	x			x			x			x			x			
Site 2			x					x					x			
Site 3				x				x				x				
...																

Figure 5.3: Service Table

for 12 hours and that a service delivery takes 1 hour. Therefore, each day is divided into 12 time periods. A cross marks a service period and an empty field indicates a non-service period. In this service table, each service occurs after its latest possible delivery time. For instance, the maximum distance between services is equal to 3 time periods for site 1.

5.2.5 Work Time Regulations

All service duties have to obey work time regulations in resemblance to German Law on Working Hours (Halbach and Menzel (2000)). In this thesis all service duties must obey the following work time regulations:

A *work time* w_{break}= 6 hours requires a break of 0.5 hours, i.e., it is not allowed to work more than 6 hours without having a break.

The *earliest time for a break* is after the first service delivery.

The *maximum number of breaks* is limited to 1 break/duty.

The *maximum work time* is limited to w_{max}= 8 hours.

The *minimum paid work time* w_{min}= 5 hours must be paid per duty, i.e., if a service crew member works less than 5 hours, he or she is paid 5 hours.

All results of the numerical experiments in Chapter 8 are based on these rules.

5.2.6 Cost of a Service Crew Schedule

Our objective is to find a crew schedule that minimizes total cost over a finite planning horizon H. The relevant costs of a solution are service duty cost and future cost:

The *service duty cost* c_s consists of the cost of all service duties based on labor cost and travel cost:

- *Labor cost* c_l is proportional to work time, which consists of service time, travel time, and waiting time. Break time is not part of work time and is not paid. If the length of a service duty is less than the minimum paid labor time, the labor cost is equal to the minimum paid labor cost.

- *Travel cost* c_t is the cost of the vehicle that is used to travel from the depot to the sites and between the sites. Travel cost includes gasoline, maintenance, capital cost, and depreciation of the vehicle and is proportional to the distance traveled.

Future cost is used to include the effect of the decisions made during the planning horizon on future periods into the objective function. We use a similar approach as Dror et al. (1985) and Dror and Ball (1987) to quantify future cost. We first determine the average labor plus transportation cost of filling a demand in the current planning period, $\bar{c}$. Then, we determine the differences in the states at the beginning and the end of the planning period, $\Delta = \sum_{m \in M}(D_m^H - D_m^0)$, and estimate future cost as $\bar{c}\Delta$.

5.3 Effect of Shifting on Crew Schedule

The main idea of the service routing problem is the shifting of service deliveries to the optimal periods. The shifting of the service deliveries to another period can lead to cost savings. Figure 5.4 shows an example with two sites.

Without shifting, each site is serviced at the latest service times by a dedicated service crew member. Besides traveling from the depot to the sites and back to the depot, the service crew members do not travel. If we would require that service must take place at the latest service times, then this solution would be optimal. If we allow services to be shifted, then alternative solutions are feasible.

Figure 5.4 shows a possible shifting, where the first service of site 2 is shifted by one hour. Because the first service is shifted, the latest service time of the second service is one hour earlier than without shifting. With shifting, the latest service times of sites 1 and 2 are different and one service crew member can service both sites. Besides traveling from the depot to the sites and back, the service crew member is traveling between the sites. Travel cost with shifting is higher than without, but only one service crew member is required, resulting in lower total work time.

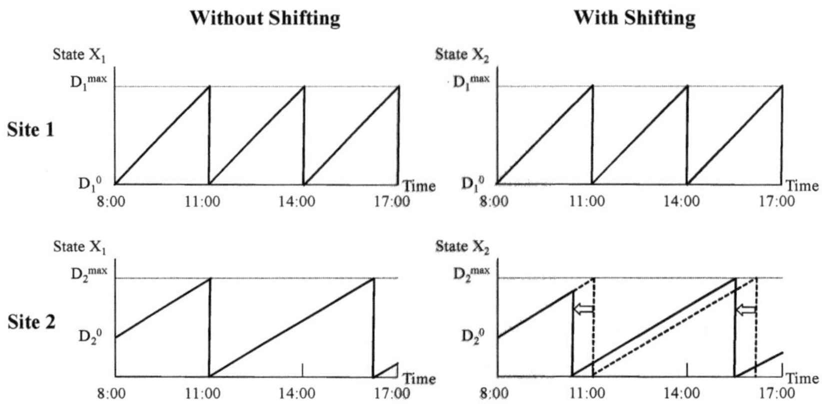

Figure 5.4: Effect of Shifting on State

Figure 5.5 illustrates the resulting crew schedules for both cases. The example illustrates the importance of considering the shifting of service times to optimize crew scheduling cost.

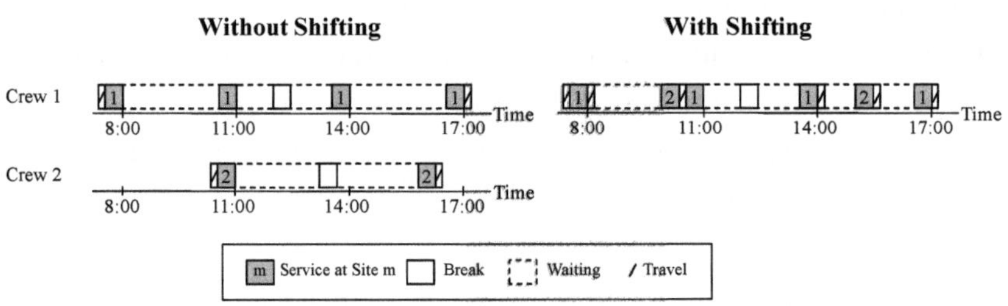

Figure 5.5: Effect of Shifting on Crew Schedule

6 Crew Scheduling and Shifting Module

Based on the fundamental basics of Chapter 2 - 4 and the challenges of Chapter 5, we develop solution approaches to solve the service routing problem. The general approach is illustrated in Figure 6.1.

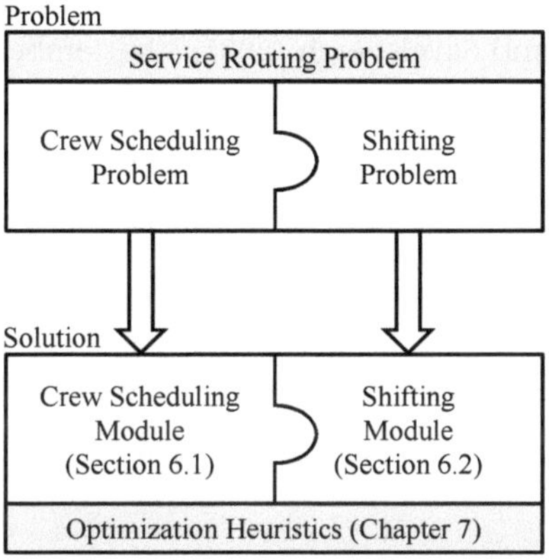

Figure 6.1: General Solution Approach for the Service Routing Problem

We decompose the service routing problem into two subproblems: a service routing problem with fixed service periods and a service table optimization problem. The service routing problem with fixed service periods can be modeled as a crew scheduling problem. We design a crew scheduling module that solves this crew scheduling problem optimally. The optimization of service tables by shifting service periods is defined as a shifting problem. For this problem, we introduce a shifting module that identifies the best local shift of a service period s at site m. The shifting module uses the crew scheduling module to determine the cost of each possible shift. To deter-

N. Holtvogt, *The Service Routing Problem*, Edition KWV,
https://doi.org/10.1007/978-3-658-24126-1_6

mine the optimal service table that results in the lowest crew scheduling cost, optimization heuristics are developed in Chapter 7.

In this chapter, Section 6.1 develops a crew scheduling module by adapting the branch-and-price approach presented in Chapter 3. Then, Section 6.2 designs the shifting module by introducing the best local shift algorithm.

6.1 Crew Scheduling Module

For fixed service periods, the service routing problem can be considered as a crew scheduling problem. The crew scheduling module solves this problem to optimality by a branch-and-price algorithm. We adapt the branch-and-price algorithm of Barnhart et al. (1998a) and Savelsbergh (2001), that embeds column generation in a branch-and-bound tree, i.e., at every node of the branch-and-bound tree possible routes for the service crew are generated. The service routing problem with fixed delivery times is decomposed into a master problem and a subproblem. The master problem is formulated as a set partitioning problem and builds a cost minimal schedule for the service crew from a subset of possible routes generated in the subproblem. In each column generation iteration, we consider a reasonable subset of columns and solve a LP-relaxation of the master problem which leads to the RMP. The RMP is solved by the simplex method.

We design the subproblem as a shortest path problem with resource constraints (Desrosiers et al. (1995)). We model the delivery time windows as nodes in the graph and adapt the dynamic programming algorithm of Desrosiers et al. (1995) by using a node selection process in a directed acyclic graph. If the subproblem cannot identify columns with negative reduced cost, the LP-relaxation of the master problem is optimal. To find integer solutions, we adapt the branching rule of Foster and Ryan (1981). The crew scheduling module terminates with an optimal solution for the current service table, such that all work regulations are fulfilled at minimum cost.

6.1.1 Master Problem

In the following, the master problem for the service routing problem is described. First, the description of the mathematical model including the restricted master problem and the generation of an initial feasible solution is given. Then, the selection of the subproblem and the process of column generation is explained. The section closes with the representation of the steps of the branch-and-price algorithm to find optimal integer solutions.

6.1.1.1 Mathematical Model

For each day of the planning horizon, the optimal schedule is determined for a given service table. A service table provides fixed service periods, which represent the service deliveries that have to be fulfilled. The set of all required service deliveries is denoted by I. The objective is to cover all service deliveries at minimal cost, i.e., to find an optimal schedule with service duties that cover all service periods. The set of all feasible service duties is denoted by J. The binary variables a_{ij} denote whether a service duty $j \in J$ covers a service delivery $i \in I$. If $a_{ij} = 1$, then the service delivery i is part of service duty j and if $a_{ij} = 0$, then the service delivery i is no part of duty j. The cost of a service duty $j \in J$ is given by c_j and includes all relevant cost of the duty. Contrary, the binary variable x_j is an indicator whether duty j is part of the solution schedule or not. If $x_j = 1$, then service delivery j is part of the solution and if $x_j = 0$, then j is no part of the solution.

The service routing problem can be formulated as a set partitioning problem:

$$\min \quad \sum_{j \in J} c_j x_j \tag{6.1}$$

$$s.t. \quad \sum_{j \in J} a_{ij} x_j = 1 \qquad \forall i \in I \tag{6.2}$$

$$x_j \in \{0,1\} \qquad \forall j \in J. \tag{6.3}$$

LP-Relaxation and Restricted Master Problem Requiring x_j to be binary and the generation of all possible service duties J can lead to high computational effort (Barnhart et al. (1998b)). Therefore, the LP-relaxation of the master problem is considered, i.e., Equations (6.3) of the master problem are relaxed to $x_j \in [0,1]$. After the determination of an optimal solution of the LP-relaxation, the optimal integer solution is obtained by the help of a branch-and-price approach (Section 6.1.1.3). Furthermore, only a subset of possible service duties $J' \subset J$ is considered in the RMP. The RMP of the master problem is as follows:

$$\min \quad \sum_{j \in J'} c_j x_j \tag{6.4}$$

$$s.t. \quad \sum_{j \in J'} a_{ij} x_j = 1 \qquad \forall i \in I \tag{6.5}$$

$$x_j \in [0,1] \qquad \forall j \in J'. \tag{6.6}$$

In this thesis, the RMP is solved by the help of the dual simplex method.

Generation of Initial Feasible Solution To start the column generation process, a set J' of service duties is needed that covers all service deliveries. To generate such an initial feasible solution, dummy service duties are introduced. For each service delivery $i \in I$, exactly one service duty is generated that covers only the corresponding duty. To make sure that a dummy duty will not be part of the optimal solution, the associated cost will be set to a very high value so that it is not profitable. The high cost results in high dual values and consequently the dummy duties are replaced in the basis by other duties with lower cost.

6.1.1.2 Column Management

In the following, the column management of this thesis is described. After the description which columns generated in the subproblem become part of the set of columns for the RMP, the storage of columns in the solution process is explained.

Selection Process During the generation of columns in the subproblem, in most cases more than one column with negative reduced cost is identified. That means that there are multiple columns that may reduce the current optimal solution of the RMP. To decrease the number of subproblem calls, *multiple pricing* is applied, i.e., not only one column is added to the RMP but multiple. To perform multiple pricing three approaches have been introduced by Lavoie et al. (1988):

1. Any column with negative reduced cost is chosen.
2. A predetermined number $pn \in \mathbb{N}^+$ of columns with highest negative reduced cost is chosen. If there are less than pn columns with negative reduced cost, all columns are added to the RMP.
3. Any column with reduced cost that is lower than a given upper bound is chosen.

Similar to Albers (2009), the second approach works best for our problem instances. Extensive computational experiments showed that the choice of $pn = 1,000$ is reasonable for all test scenarios of the thesis. The approach leads to acceptable computational time for all test cases.

Storage Process We want to add the pn columns with the highest negative reduced cost to the RMP. For an efficient storage of relevant columns, the set of columns J' of the RMP is saved as a sequence of arcs. Using the arcs, the sequence of activities can be derived for the duties of the optimal integer solution. By applying this approach, memory requirements can be kept low.

During the column generation process, the duties are ranked by their negative reduced cost. Since only pn columns will be added to the RMP, only a maximum of pn columns are stored during the column generation process of the subproblem. When the number of columns with negative reduced cost has reached the upper limit pn, it is checked whether the negative reduced cost of the next generated column is lower than the least negative reduced cost in the ranked list. If it is lower, the column with the least reduced cost is deleted and the new one is ranked into the list. Thus, only a maximum of pn columns are stored during each subproblem call.

6.1.1.3 Optimal Integer Solutions

The optimal solution of the RMP is typically not integer but consists of multiple fractional variables. Branch-and-price will be applied to find the optimal integer solution.

An upper bound for the cost of the optimal integer schedule is helpful to avoid the exploration of unprofitable branches. The lower bound is already given by the solution of the LP-relaxation. The following section starts with the description of the determination of an upper bound by variable fixing and closes with the explanation of the branch-and-price approach.

Initial Upper Bound To determine an initial upper bound for the branch-and-price approach, we adapt the variable fixing introduced in Section 3.3.2. Figure 6.2 illustrates the general approach of this thesis for the determination of the upper bound.

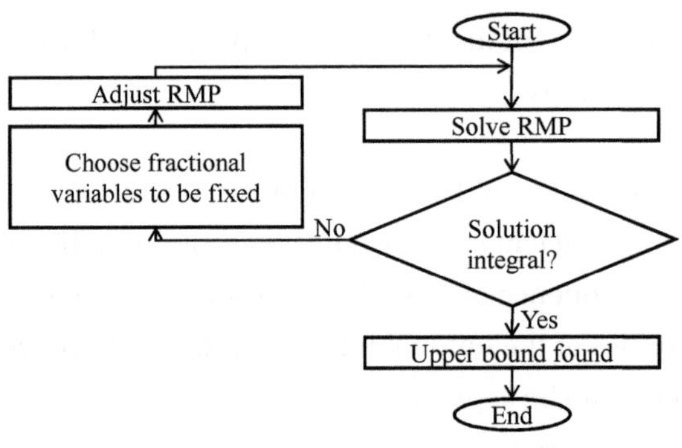

Figure 6.2: Initial Upper Bound

After finding the optimal solution of the RMP, it is checked whether the solution is already integral. If it is integral, no upper bound is needed, because we have found the optimal integer solution. In case of a fractional solution, we determine fractional variables x_j to be fixed. The variables are added as constraints $x_j = 1$ to the RMP. The column generation process to solve the RMP starts again. To avoid the generation of useless duties in the subproblem, the service deliveries that are already covered due to the variable fixing are excluded from the subproblem. If the solution of the adjusted RMP is again fractional, further fractional variables are set to 1 and the resulting RMP is optimized. The process terminates after the determination of an integer solution of the RMP. This solution represents the initial upper bound for our branch-and-price approach.

A big challenge of variable fixing is the choice of the fractional variables that are set to 1. This choice can influence the solution quality. Figure 6.3 shows how the fractional variables are determined in this thesis. n_{fix} denotes the number of variables that should be fixed. After the determination of the optimal fractional solution of the RMP, all fractional variables x_j are stored in a list N_{frac}. A variable x_j corresponds to a service duty that covers one or more service deliveries. The variable fixing cost c_j of a fractional variable x_j is determined by $1 - frac_{x_j}$, with $frac_{x_j}$ denoting the fractional value of x_j in the optimal solution of the RMP. The variable x_j with the lowest variable fixing cost is fixed, i.e, $x_j = 1$. Then, x_j is deleted from list N_{frac}, i.e., $N_{frac} = N_{frac} \setminus \{x_j\}$. All elements in N_{frac} that cover at least one of the service deliveries already covered by x_j are deleted from N_{frac} as well. If the number of fixed

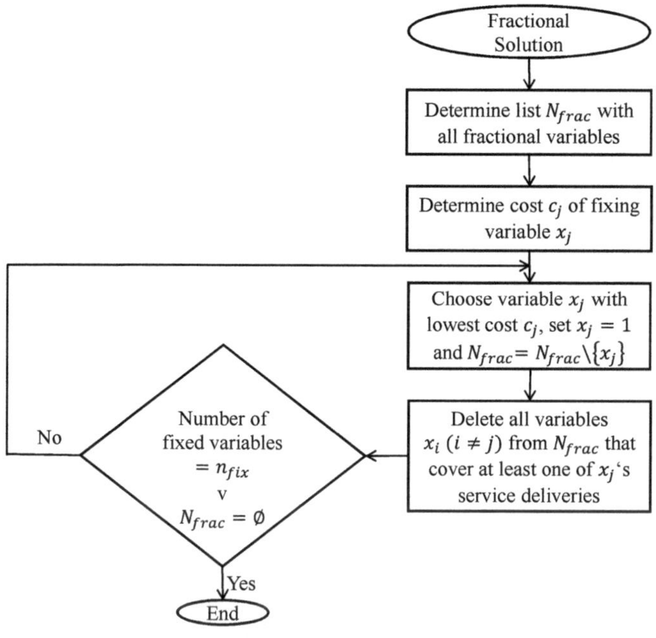

Figure 6.3: Choice of Fractional Variables

variables is equal to n_{fix} or the list N_{frac} of fractional variables is empty, then the variable fixing is terminated. Otherwise, the process is repeated by choosing again the fractional variable with the lowest cost of variable fixing in list N_{frac}. Our computational experiments showed that the choice of $n_{fix} = 10$ leads to a reasonable initial upper bound with low computational effort.

Branch-and-Price We determined a lower bound by the solution of the LP-relaxation and an initial upper bound by variable fixing. Now, we focus on the branch-and-price algorithm. In this approach, column generation is embedded in a branch-and-bound tree, i.e., column generation is performed at every branch and provides the cost of the RMP of the specific branch.

The solution process of the RMP at each branch starts with a set of feasible columns, which speeds up the column generation process and consequently the branch-and-price approach. Figure 6.4 illustrates the steps after solving the RMP at a branch. The cost resulting from a branch is compared to the current upper bound. If

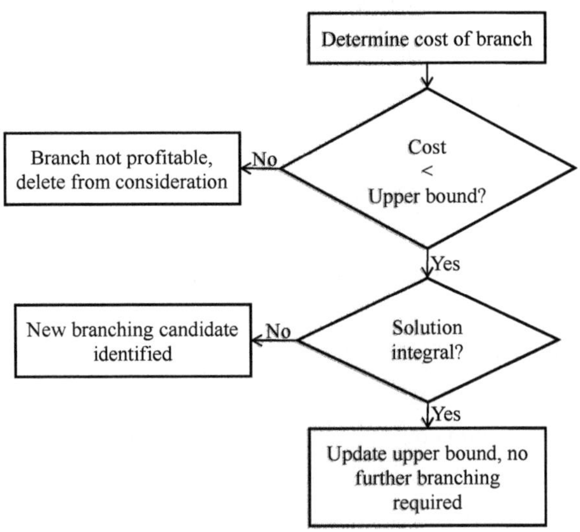

Figure 6.4: Branching Decisions

the cost is greater than the upper bound, the branch is not profitable and the branch is excluded from further examinations. If the cost is lower than the upper bound, it is checked whether the solution is integral. If the solution is integral, it marks the new upper bound and no further branches at this node are required. If the solution is not integral, new branching candidates at the corresponding node have to be identified. The branch-and-price process terminates when no more branching candidates are available. The current upper bound marks the optimal integer solution.

The general branching approach of this thesis is based on the approach of Foster and Ryan (1981): Assume that the fractional solution of the RMP contains the two service duties k and h with the fractional decision variables x_k and x_h. Duty k covers

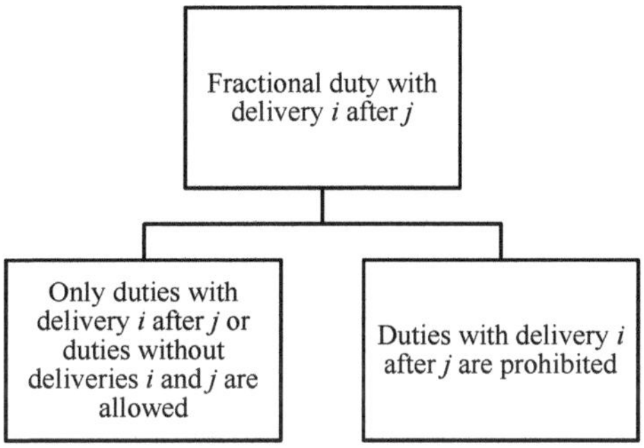

Figure 6.5: Branching Approach

service deliveries i and j, but duty h covers only one service delivery i or j. Then, the left branch contains only duties that contain service delivery i and j or neither of them. However, the right branch contains only one of the duties or neither of them.

We adapt this approach in accordance to Malcherek (2010). Figure 6.5 illustrates the general branching method of this thesis. In the left branch, delivery i is always after j and the right branch prohibits this sequence of deliveries. In both cases, duties that do not contain neither delivery i nor j, are always included. The branches are easy to realize due to the representation of the service deliveries in a connection network. An arc from delivery j to delivery i represents the direct connection between the two deliveries and indicates that delivery i is after delivery j. Figures 6.6 and 6.7 illustrate the approach. To enforce this sequence in the left branch, all arcs originat-

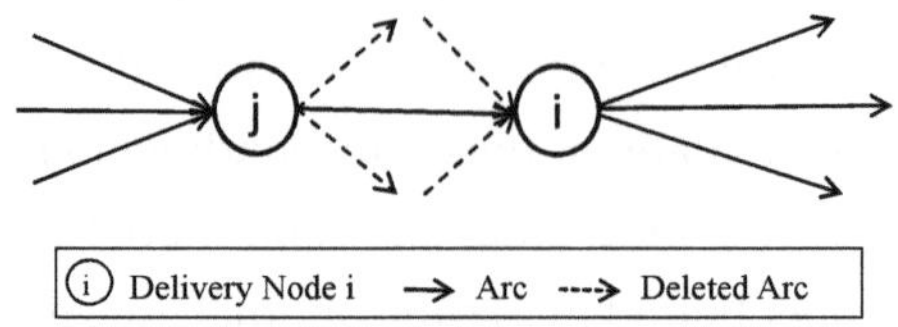

Figure 6.6: Left Branch of Branching Approach

ing from node j are deleted apart from the arc to node i (Figure 6.6). For the right branch, the arc from node j to node i is deleted and all other arcs originating from node j are kept (Figure 6.7).

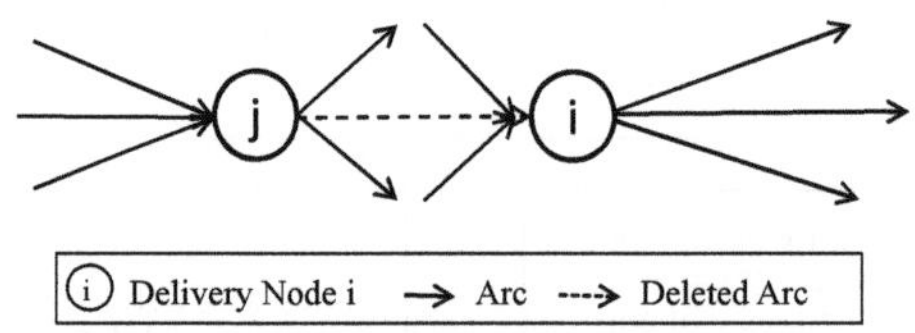

Figure 6.7: Right Branch of Branching Approach

To utilize the columns already generated for the lower bound and other branches, the set J'' of already generated columns is adjusted for each branch. For instance, we assign to the left branch the set of columns $J'_{left} \subseteq J''$. J'_{left} contains all columns of J'' that represent duties where delivery i is after j or where neither delivery j nor i is covered.

We developed a procedure to decide on the next branching candidate. First, the branch with the lowest cost of the non-integral solution of the RMP is chosen. The low cost of the fractional solution indicates the potential of low cost of the resulting integral solution. Second, the fractional variables of the corresponding solution are considered and ordered with increasing size. A high fractional value may indicate that the corresponding duty is desirable for the solution. Then, the duty with the largest fractional variable is chosen. The first connection from one service delivery to another service delivery of this duty is the next branch. Experiments with different approaches showed that this approach delivers the optimal integer solution within acceptable computational time for the test scenarios of this thesis.

6.1.2 Generation of Service Duties in Subproblem

In the subproblem, new feasible duties with negative reduced cost are generated. The corresponding columns are added to the set of columns J' of the RMP. In the following, we describe the generation of service duties in the subproblem.

In Section 6.1.2.1, we model the connections of different activities in a connection network. The arcs represent connections and the nodes represent activities at a certain site. Only feasible connections are constructed such that a feasible path in the network represents a feasible service duty. Section 6.1.2.2 describes the approach to identify feasible paths with negative reduced in the connection network.

6.1.2.1 Network Construction

Before we can identify feasible service duties, we have to decide on an appropriate network representation. In Section 3.2.2.2, we introduced a time-line and a connection network. In a time-line network representation, tasks are represented by arcs. In this thesis, tasks take place at different locations and tasks do not include trips. Therefore, each task is associated with the time to drive from one site to another site. The paths from one task to all other tasks have to be connected to each task. This leads to more than one arc for each task what complicates a clear network representation. Another disadvantage of this representation is that infeasible connections cannot be excluded explicitly in the construction process.

In a connection network representation, tasks are modeled as nodes. The number of arcs can be immense, in particular if the sequence of tasks is highly flexible, which is very common for the service routing problem. For n nodes, the connection network consists of $\mathcal{O}(n^2)$ arcs (Albers (2009)). But the representation involves multiple advantages, e.g., it captures complex relations between different tasks and models all feasible connections. In total, this representation enables us to model the network structure of the service routing problem better than the time-line network.

Consequently, we identify feasible service duties by formulating the SPPRC on a connection network. According to Section 3.2.2.1, we define the network as graph $G(V,A)$ with node set V and arc set A. The set of nodes $V = N \cup \{o, d\}$ and arcs A result from the service table of the underlying problem. First, the nodes are generated and then the feasible connections between the nodes are constructed.

Node Construction N is the set of nodes that can be visited by a path p with origin o and destination d. The service routing problem deals with a total of four different node types. Since each service duty has to start and end at a single depot, o and d represent the depot as *start depot node* and *end depot node*. The set N consists of the set of *delivery nodes* N_D and the set of *break nodes* N_B. Table 6.1 gives an overview of the four node types.

Node Type	Characteristic
Start Depot Node	origin of each path through network
End Depot Node	destination of each path through network
Delivery Node	service delivery that has to be covered
Break Node	optional breaks

Table 6.1: Overview of Node Types

The *start depot node* is the start and the *end depot node* is the end of each path through the network.

A *delivery node* results from a service period of the service table. For each service period a node is generated with the information about the corresponding time period and site of the service due. Each delivery node has to be covered exactly once after the solution of the RMP. During the generation of service duties, a delivery node can be covered by more than one generated duty.

A *break node* is constructed in dependence of each delivery node. Every time a delivery node $i \in N_D$ is generated, a corresponding break node $i_B \in N_B$ is generated for the same site associated with a start time right after the end of the service of the corresponding delivery node. This ensures that in the generation process of feasible paths breaks are also considered. This approach is possible, because a service crew member is allowed to take a break at each site. The break nodes are only optional nodes, i.e., a break node does not need to be covered after the solution of the RMP. During the generation process of feasible duties, it is checked if a break is required according to the work time regulations (see Section 5.2.5).

Arc Construction After the generation of nodes, the connections are modeled as arcs. The construction process considers only feasible arcs. Depending on the different node types, different outgoing and incoming arcs are possible. The end of an arc is referred to as *tail node*.

Figure 6.8 illustrates all possible incoming and outgoing arcs for the four node types. Since the start depot node represents the origin for each path, there exist only

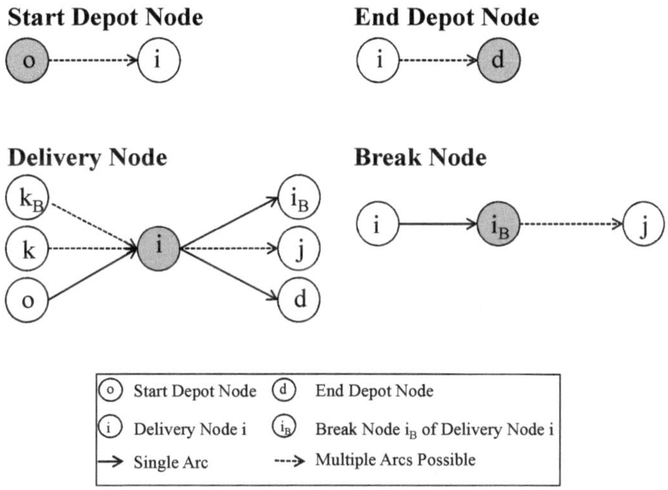

Figure 6.8: Incoming and Outgoing Arcs for Different Node Types

outgoing arcs. It is not possible to start a service duty with a break or to end it directly after the start. Consequently, all outgoing arcs represent connections from the start depot node to delivery nodes. On the contrary, the end depot node has only incoming arcs. Since it is not allowed to end a service duty with a break, all incoming arcs represent only connections from delivery nodes.

Delivery nodes can be connected with all types of nodes. For each delivery node, there exists exactly one connection from the start depot node and one to the end depot node. Multiple arcs represent the possible connections from and to other delivery nodes. For each delivery node, exactly one break node is generated. The only incoming arc of a break node originates at its corresponding delivery node. The outgoing arcs of a break node are connected to all delivery nodes that are successors of its corresponding delivery node. Hence, for the delivery nodes, there exist three different types of incoming arcs and three different arcs of outgoing arcs.

A break node is always modeled after its corresponding delivery node, but the node can be connected to all other delivery nodes. A direct connection from a break node to the depot nodes is not allowed, because a service crew member can only have a break before or after a service delivery. Consequently, a break node has only one incoming node representing the connection from the associated delivery node and multiple outgoing arcs representing connections to other delivery nodes.

Algorithm 6.1 determines the arcs based on the given set of nodes V. At the beginning the set of arcs A is empty. The algorithm starts with the construction of all arcs from the start depot node $o \in V$ to all delivery nodes $i \in N_D$ (lines (2) - (6)). Each connection (o, i) is added to the set of arcs A (line (4)). In lines (7) - (11), all connections from all delivery nodes to the end depot node are considered and added as arc (i, d) to set A (line (9)). Then, the delivery nodes are considered as head node (lines (12) - (18)). A delivery node $i \in N_D$ is connected to all reachable delivery nodes to generate feasible connections. A node j is reachable if the end of the service period of the predecessor node end_i including the travel time t_{ij} is less than or equal to the starting time of the service period of the tail node $start_j$, i.e., it must be guaranteed that the service crew member arrives before or at the starting time of the service period of the next service delivery (line (14)). The feasible connections (i, j) are added as arcs to set A. Since not only delivery nodes have to be considered as tail nodes, all feasible connections from delivery nodes to break nodes have been constructed. Finally, the connections from break nodes to delivery nodes are generated (lines (23) - (29)). Also the break nodes are only connected to delivery nodes that are reachable (line (25)).

Algorithm 6.1 Arc Construction

Require: $V = N_D \cup N_B \cup \{o, d\}$

$A = \emptyset$
for $o \in V$ **do**
    for all $i \in N_D$ **do**
        $A := A \cup \{(o, i)\}$
    end for
end for
for $d \in V$ **do**
    for all $i \in N_D$ **do**
        $A := A \cup \{(i, d)\}$
    end for
end for
for all $i \in N_D$ **do**
    for all $j \in N_D$ **do**
        if $end_i + t_{ij} \leq start_j$ **then**
            $A := A \cup \{(i, j)\}$
        end if
    end for
end for
for all $i \in N_D$ **do**
    find corresponding $i_B \in N_B$
    $A := A \cup \{(i, i_B)\}$
end for
for all $i_B \in N_B$ **do**
    for all $j \in N_D$ **do**
        if $end_{i_B} + t_{i_B j} \leq start_j$ **then**
            $A := A \cup \{(i_B, j)\}$
        end if
    end for
end for

The generated arcs are added to the set of arcs A (line (26)).

To identify feasible paths through the connection network, the arcs are associated with service time, break time, travel time, driving distance, and reduced cost influenced by the corresponding dual variable. Table 6.2 gives an overview of the information depending on the different arc types. Generally, each arc provides information

	Service Time of Tail Node	Break Time of Tail Node	Travel Time/Distance Head Node to Tail Node	Reduced Cost Influenced by Dual Variable
Start Depot Node -> Delivery Node	√		√	√
Delivery Node -> End Depot Node			√	
Delivery Node -> Delivery Node	√		(√)	√
Delivery Node -> Break Node		√		
Break Node -> Delivery Node	√		(√)	√

Table 6.2: Overview of Arc Types

on the duration of travel from one node to another node and on the duration of servicing the tail node. Arcs from the start depot node $o \in A$ to delivery nodes contain the service times at the delivery nodes, the travel times and distances from the start depot node to the delivery nodes. In addition, the arcs are linked to the reduced cost resulting from the tail nodes. The reduced cost of an arc (i, j) results from the associated optimization cost c_{ij} and the dual variable π_i that corresponds to service delivery i. The dual variable is associated with Constraints (6.5) of the RMP that ensures that service delivery i is covered exactly once. The reduced cost is then determined by $\bar{c}_{oi} = c_{oi} - \pi_i$.

Connections from a delivery node $i \in N_D$ to the end depot node $d \in A$ contain travel times and distances between the head node and the tail node. The reduced cost is equal to the optimization cost associated with arc (i, d), because the tail node corresponds to no delivery associated with Constraints (6.5).

Arcs from delivery nodes to delivery nodes include service times of tail nodes and the reduced cost is influenced by the dual variable of the tail node π_j, i.e., for arc (i, j) the reduced cost are determined by $\bar{c}_{ij} = c_{ij} - \pi_j$. Since connections between delivery nodes with the same sites are allowed, only arcs with different sites as head and tail node contain travel times and distances.

The connections from delivery nodes to their associated break nodes result only in break times. However, the arcs from break nodes to delivery nodes contain service times of the tail nodes and reduced cost influenced by the corresponding reduced variable. If the break node and the delivery node are connected to different sites, travel times and distances are included.

6.1.2.2 Service Duty Generation

We next describe the approach to identify feasible paths with negative reduced cost. These paths represent the service duties that are added as columns to the RMP. First, we specify the depth-first search through the network to find paths. Second, we describe how labels are determined and how the feasibility of a connection is checked during the search. Finally, we determine feasible paths with negative reduced cost based on labels at the end depot node.

Search Algorithm The determination of paths through a network can be based on a breadth-first or a depth-first search. The *breadth-first search* determines paths through a tree by examining one level after another level. The search starts with the examination of the nodes on the top level. Then, the next levels are analyzed sequentially. The search stops with the nodes at the bottom level, the leaf nodes (Sedgewick (2002)). The *depth-first search* determines paths through a tree by examining one branch after another (Tarjan (1972)). After reaching the leaf node of the first branch, the next branch is examined.

For our branch-and-price approach, we only need the pn paths with the lowest cost. The profitability can only be determined for complete paths. Therefore, it is efficient to determine complete paths as fast as possible to neglect unprofitable paths. The memory requirements of breadth-first search are very high, because most of the incomplete paths need to be saved in parallel. That can already lead to excess memory consumption for mid-sized graphs.

To keep memory requirements at a low level, we determine paths based on a depth-first search. In contrast to a breadth-first search, no incomplete paths are buffered in parallel. Figure 6.9 illustrates the general idea of our approach by an example. We use

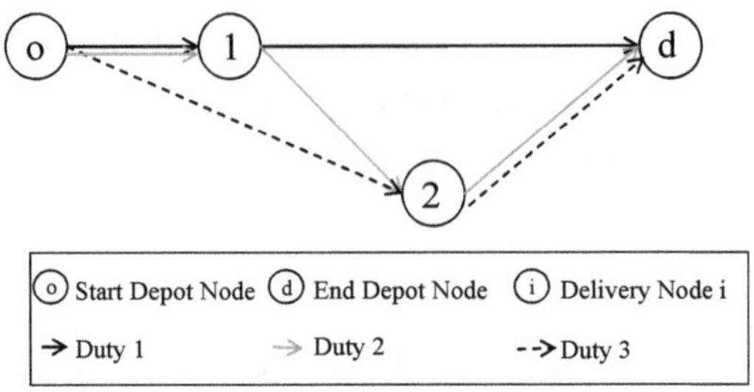

Figure 6.9: Duty Generation - Depth-First Search

a connection network with a start and end depot node as well as two delivery nodes 1 and 2. We ignore possible break nodes. We assume a total of 5 arcs: two from the start depot node (one to node 1 and one to 2), one from node 1 to node 1, and two to the end depot node (one from node 1 and one from node 2 node). We start the search for paths at the start depot node and choose the first outgoing arc. The arc connects the start depot node with delivery node 1. Again, we choose the first outgoing arc. The arc's tail node is the end depot node. The first path has been determined. We go back to delivery node 1 and consider the next outgoing arc to delivery node 2. Then, we take the first outgoing arc of delivery node 2. The tail node is the end depot node and the second path has been found. We examine again the head node of the current arc, delivery node 2. Since there are no more unconsidered outgoing arcs, we go to the predecessor node, i.e., delivery node 1. There are no more outgoing arcs we have not analyzed yet and we move back to the start depot node. We take the next outgoing arc to delivery node 2. Again delivery node 2 is appraised, the outgoing arc to the end depot node is considered, and we get the third path through the network. We go back to delivery node 2 and find no more outgoing arcs. Therefore, we go back to the start depot node. As there are no outgoing arcs left, the search is completed.

The subproblem of our service routing problem involves the solution of a SPPRC

(Section 3.3.3). Therefore, the depth-first search terminates the examination of a branch if a certain constraint is violated. Thus, it is ensured that only feasible paths will be generated.

Algorithm 6.2 describes the depth-first search in general. We are given a set of nodes V and a set of arcs A. The maximum number of columns to be added to the RMP is denoted by pn. At the beginning, the set of *labels* to be examined and the set of new columns J_{new} are empty. A label is connected with a certain arc and contains the information of the corresponding path to this arc. A detailed description of labels is given below.

The algorithm starts with the start depot node $o \in V$. The labels L_o for the outgoing arcs A_o of the start depot node are determined and are added to the set of labels to be examined. This set is denoted by L. An empty set L indicates that all outgoing arcs have already been considered (lines (4)-(7)). Thus, the search terminates. Otherwise, the first label $l_{curr} \in L$ is chosen and the corresponding arc a_{curr} is determined. Since each label will be examined exactly once, it is removed from set L (line (9)). Then, the tail node n of arc a_{curr} is determined and it is analyzed whether the connection leads to a feasible path. If the connection is not feasible, the search moves to the next label of L. Details on the feasibility check are given below.

If n is equal to the end depot node d, we have reached the leaf node of the branch and can decide whether the corresponding duty is added to the set of new columns J_{new} or not (lines (12)-(22)). If the set of new columns J_{new} to be added to the RMP has not reached the maximum number of columns pn, duty j is added to J_{new} and the search continues with the next label, if L is not empty (line (5)). If the maximum number of columns pn is reached, it is checked whether the reduced cost $\bar{c}_j$ of the new duty j is higher than the reduced cost of the duty k in J_{new} with the least negative reduced cost $\bar{c}_k$. The column with the least negative reduced cost indicates the smallest cost decrease in the RMP. Thus, if the reduced cost of duty j is higher, duty k is replaced by duty j in the set of new columns J_{new} and we move to line (5). If the reduced cost of duty j is lower than the reduced cost of duty k, duty j is neglected and we move again to line (5).

If the tail node of the current arc a_{curr} is not the end depot node, the labels L_n for the outgoing arcs A_n of the tail node n are determined based on the predecessor la-

Algorithm 6.2 Service Duty Generation

Require: V, A, p

1: $L = \emptyset$, $J_{new} = \emptyset$
2: start with $o \in V$
3: determine labels L_o for outgoing arcs $A_o \subset A$ of $o \in V$
4: $L := L_o$
5: **if** $L = \emptyset$ **then**
6:     return J_{new}
7: **end if**
8: choose $l_{curr} \in L$ and determine corresponding arc a_{curr}
9: $L := L \setminus \{l_{curr}\}$
10: determine tail node $n \in V$ of a_{curr}
11: **if** connection feasible **then**
12:     **if** $n = d$ **then**
13:         determine duty j
14:         **if** $|J_{new}| < pn$ **then**
15:             $J_{new} := J_{new} \cup \{j\}$
16:         **else**
17:             search duty $k \in J_{new}$ with $\bar{c}_k = \max\{\bar{c}_i | i \in J_{new}\}$
18:             **if** $\bar{c}_j < \bar{c}_k$ **then**
19:                 $J_{new} := J_{new} \setminus \{k\}$
20:                 $J_{new} := J_{new} \cup \{j\}$
21:             **end if**
22:         **end if**
23:     **else**
24:         determine labels L_n for outgoing arcs $A_n \subset A$ of $n \in V$ based on l_{curr}
25:         $L := L \cup L_n$
26:     **end if**
27: **end if**
28: go to 5

bel l_{curr}. The corresponding labels are added to set L. Then, we move back to line (5) and check whether L is empty. If not, we continue with the search of new feasible paths. Otherwise, the search terminates with the best found feasible duties.

Label Determination Algorithm 6.2 determines feasible paths by labels. Each time a path is expanded, a label is determined. Each label contains the information of the path including the information about the connected tail node. At the beginning, all variables associated with the start depot node are equal to 0.

Our approach to determine labels is an adaption of the label-pulling approach described in Section 3.3.3. Figure 6.10 illustrates how a label is determined based on a simple example on travel time. The arc to be considered represents the connection

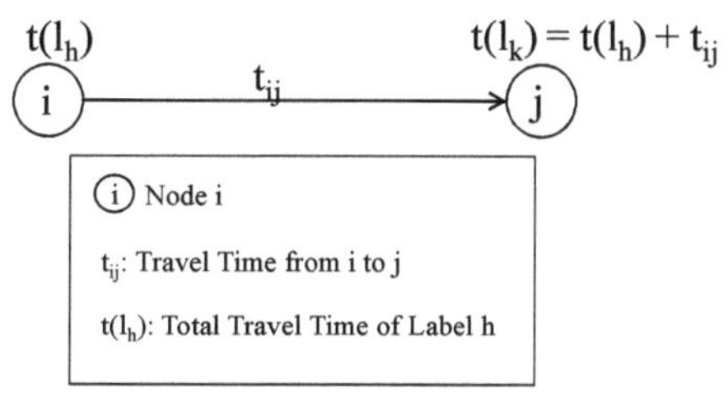

Figure 6.10: Determination of Label - Travel Time

from node i to node j and the travel time between the nodes is denoted by t_{ij}. Node i is already associated with label l_h and includes the travel time of the path to the node denoted by $t(l_h)$. We expand the path by the connection to node j and determine a new label l_k. The travel time associated with the label is denoted by the travel time of the predecessor label and the travel time from node i to j, i.e., $t(l_k) = t(l_h) + t_{ij}$.

The labels require multiple variables to determine the cost, the feasibility, or the detailed schedule of a path. The different variables can be divided into two groups. The variables for the first group can be determined for each label comparable to the example with travel time (Figure 6.10). The determination of the second group's variables requires more information and may differ for different node types.

The following variables are determined based on the variables of the predecessor label and the variables associated with the corresponding arc:

The *travel time* is explicitly given by the predecessor label and the arc that expands the corresponding path (Figure 6.10). The travel time is important to determine the total work time of a path.

The *driving distance* of the new label is also determined by adding the driving distance of the associated arc to the driving distance of the predecessor label. The driving distance of a path enables us to determine the corresponding travel cost.

Each label contains the information about its direct *predecessor label.* That enables us to trace back all visited nodes of the corresponding path.

The determination of the following variables requires not only the information of the predecessor label and the connecting arc, but the information about the involved nodes and associated time periods as well:

The *time after service* of a label enables us to determine the detailed schedule of the corresponding path. The time is always given by the end of service or break at the tail node. If the tail node is the end depot node, the time after service is the time of the arrival at the depot and is determined by the time after service of the predecessor label and the travel time.

Besides travel time and service time, the *work time* may also include waiting times. Driving time and service time are given by the predecessor label and the corresponding arc. To decide whether waiting times have to be added or not, the following cases have to be distinguished:

- If the time after service of the predecessor label augmented by the travel time equals the starting time of service at the tail node, no waiting time is required. The work time is equal to the sum of the work time of the predecessor label, the travel time and the service time of the tail node.
- If the time after service of the predecessor label augmented by the travel time is lower than the starting time of service at the tail node, additional waiting time is required. The waiting time is given by the time between the arrival at the tail node and the starting time of service.

Note that, if waiting time is required, the *reduced cost* of a label is also adapted by the additional work time multiplied by labor cost.

The information about the *total time before break* is required to check whether a path fulfills the underlying break rules. If the tail node is a break node, the total time before break contains the information after which time period a break takes place in the corresponding path.

Feasibility Check After the determination of a new label and an associated arc, Algorithm 6.2 checks the feasibility of the resulting path (lines (8)-(11)). A path is feasible, if the resource constraints of the SPPRC are fulfilled. For the service routing problem, work time regulations provide resource constraints. Consequently, for each addition of a new connection to an existing path, the maximum work time and the break rules must be taken into account. The labels provide all relevant information for the feasibility check.

The addition of a new connection is feasible, if the resulting path fulfills one of the following requirements:

No break node is covered, the total work time is less than the maximum time until break w_{break} and the maximum work time w_{max}.

The work time is greater than the maximum time until break w_{break}, but less than the maximum work time w_{max} and a break node is covered by the corresponding path before w_{break} is reached. Furthermore, the path does not cover more than one break node.

Final Duty Determination If the search of Algorithm 6.2 reaches the end depot node d, the service duty of the corresponding path is determined based on the information of the last generated label (lines (12)-(13)). The determination of a duty is easily obtained. The main information about the total work time, travel time, driving distance, and the reduced cost are directly provided by the label. The cost c_j of a duty j results from the total work time w_j times the labor cost factor $cost_l$ and the total driving distance dd_j times the travel cost factor $cost_t$, i.e., $c_j = cost_l \times w_j + cost_t \times dd_j$.

By the help of backtracking the corresponding predecessor labels, all covered nodes are identified. The information of the time after service at each label gives the detailed times for the coverage of each node.

The labels do not explicitly contain the information about the starting time of the duty. However, based on the time after service of the first label, the starting time at the start depot node is determined by subtracting the service time at the first node and the travel time from the time after service.

In case that the total work time is less than the minimum paid work time w_{min}, the work time, the reduced cost, and the optimization cost of the duty have to be adapted. Then, the total work time is set equal to the minimum paid work time. The reduced cost and the optimization cost are augmented by the resulting extra cost.

Finally, the information about total time before break tells us, when a break takes place. If we add this time period to the starting time at the depot, we get the starting time of the corresponding break. In case the maximum time until break restriction will not be violated, the sequence of break and driving activity is changed. That results in duties that have a break directly after arriving at the next delivery node.

6.2 Shifting Module

The previous section described how our crew scheduling module determines the optimal solution for a given service table. In the overall service routing problem, we must also determine optimal service tables. The shift of a service period results in a new service table. Our new developed shifting module determines the best local shift of a certain service period s at a certain site m by comparing the cost of various advancements and postponements of service periods. This section describes how a service at a certain site and period is shifted.

6.2.1 Local Shift

If we shift a service at site m to another period, we have to ensure that the maximum time difference between services is respected. The local shift approach ensures that the feasibility of a service table is maintained. Figure 6.11 provides an example of a local shift with one site, 7 time periods, and a maximum time difference between services of 3 service periods. In the initial table, the time difference between the service

Initial Setting

Time Period	1	2	3	4	5	6	7
Site 1	x			x			x

Shift Service of Period 4 to Period 1

Time Period	1	2	3	4	5	6	7
Site 1	x		x				x

Adapt Successor

Time Period	1	2	3	4	5	6	7
Site 1	x		x			x	

Figure 6.11: Local Shift

periods is equal to the maximum time difference between services. Then, we shift the second service from period 4 to period 3. The distance between the first and the second are 2 periods and between the second and the third 4 periods. Since the time difference between the second and the third service is higher than the maximum time difference allowed, we have to adapt the service table by shifting the third service from period 7 to period 6. This restores the feasibility of the service table and the local shift is completed.

The general approach to shift a service is as follows. Consider a service table ψ with service at site m in period s. Let the minimal cost of the table be $c(\psi)$. $c(\psi)$ is determined by our crew scheduling algorithm. Next, consider a local shift, where the service s at site m is moved by i periods to period $s+i$. We distinguish two cases: $i<0$ and $i>0$.

For $i<0$, we move the service to an earlier period. If the subsequent service period of the new service period $s+i$ at site m is after period $s+i+dis_m$, then the maximum time difference dis_m between services is exceeded. Then, we move the subsequent service to period $s+i+dis_m$. We continue by analyzing all future periods at site m and, if necessary, move services to earlier periods to ensure feasibility of the schedule. If required, we add services at the end of the planning horizon.

For $i>0$, we move the service to a later period. We essentially use the same approach as above, but might have to move some services that take place before service period s to later periods to ensure that the maximum time difference dis_m between services is not exceeded. We might have to add services at the beginning of the planning horizon.

We denote the resulting service table by $\tilde{\psi}(m,s,i)$, where the service period s of table ψ has been moved at site m by i periods. The cost of the optimal schedule of the table is $c(\tilde{\psi}(m,s,i))$ and is determined by our crew scheduling algorithm.

6.2.2 Find Best Local Shift

Based on the local shift of a service period the best local shift is determined. The general idea is to perform the local shift of a service step by step until no more cost improvements are identified and the best local shift has been found. Since we are allowed to shift service to earlier and later periods, we search the best local shift to earlier periods and to later periods respectively. Then, we compare the results for both shift directions and the one with lower cost is the best local shift. Note, that for the optimization heuristics we will develop in Chapter 7, we also want to identify neighborhood solutions that are worse than the initial solution. Therefore, the best local shift may lead to a cost increase compared to the initial solution.

Figure 6.12 illustrates a best local shift. An example of a service table with 3 sites, 7 time periods, and optimization cost of 100 € is given. We want to identify the best local shift of service period 4 at site 1. This requires a shift of the successor service from period 7 to period 6. The crew scheduling module determines the cost of 95 € for the resulting schedule. Since we found a cost decrease compared to the initial table, we continue by shifting the service to an earlier period and shift the service from period 3 to period 2 and adapt the successor. The cost of the resulting service table is greater than the cost of the previous table. Consequently, we terminate with

Algorithm 6.3 Best Local Shift

Require: $\psi, c(\psi), m, s$

1: $i^*_L(m,s) := 1$
2: **if** $c(\tilde{\psi}(m,s,-1)) \geq c(\psi)$ **then**
3:     go to 11
4: **else**
5:     $i := 2$
6:     **while** $c(\tilde{\psi}(m,s,-i)) < c(\tilde{\psi}(m,s,-i^*_L(m,s)))$ **do**
7:         $i^*_L(m,s) := i$
8:         $i := i+1$
9:     **end while**
10: **end if**
11: $i^*_R(m,s) := 1$
12: **if** $c(\tilde{\psi}(m,s,1)) \geq c(\psi)$ **then**
13:     go to 21
14: **else**
15:     $i := 2$
16:     **while** $c(\tilde{\psi}(m,s,i)) < c(\tilde{\psi}(m,s,i^*_R(m,s)))$ **do**
17:         $i^*_R(m,s) := i$
18:         $i := i+1$
19:     **end while**
20: **end if**
21: **if** $c(\tilde{\psi}(m,s,i^*_R(m,s))) < c(\tilde{\psi}(m,s,i^*_L(m,s)))$ **then**
22:     $i^*(m,s) := i^*_R(m,s)$
23: **else**
24:     $i^*(m,s) := -i^*_L(m,s)$
25: **end if**
26: return $i^*(m,s)$

Determine Cost of Initial Table:

Time Period	1	2	3	4	5	6	7
Site 1	x			x			x
Site 2				x			
Site 3					x		

Total Cost: 100 €

Determine Best Local Shift to Earlier Time Periods:

Shift to Preceding Period

Time Period	1	2	3	4	5	6	7
Site 1	x		x			x	
Site 2				x			
Site 3					x		

Total Cost: 95 €
⇒ Cost Decrease
⇒ Continue

} Best Local Shift

Shift to Next Preceding Period

Time Period	1	2	3	4	5	6	7
Site 1	x	x			x		
Site 2				x			
Site 3					x		

Total Cost: 98 €
⇒ No Cost Decrease
⇒ Shift to Successor

Determine Best Local Shift to Later Time Periods:

Shift to Successor Period

Time Period	1	2	3	4	5	6	7
Site 1		x			x		x
Site 2				x			
Site 3					x		

Total Cost: 96 €
⇒ Cost Decrease
⇒ Shift to Successor

Shift to Next Successor Period

Time Period	1	2	3	4	5	6	7
Site 1			x			x	x
Site 2				x			
Site 3					x		

Total Cost: 99 €
⇒ No Cost Decrease

Figure 6.12: Example: Best Local Shift of Service Period 4 at Site 1

the shifting to earlier periods. We have found the best local shift to earlier periods, the shift from period 4 to 3.

Next, we analyze the local shifts to later periods. Based on the initial table, we shift the service from period 4 to period 5 and adapt the service at period 1 by shifting it to period 2. The cost of the resulting service table is less than the cost of the initial table. We continue by shifting the service from period 5 to 6 and adapt the predecessor. The resulting cost is greater than the cost of the previous service table. We have already found the best local shift to later periods, the shift from period 4 to period 5.

Next, we compare the cost of the best local shift to earlier periods to the one to later periods. As the cost for the best local shift to earlier periods has minimal cost, it marks the best local solution, i.e., the shift to period 3 is the best local shift of the service in period 4.

Algorithm 6.3 describes the general best local shift algorithm. For a given site m and service period s, we want to find the best local shift $i^*(m,s)$. Our best local shift algorithm starts by analyzing the cost of shifting the service period to the preceding period, period $s-1$ (line (2)). If $c(\tilde{\psi}(m,s,-1))$ is less than $c(\psi)$, i.e., if the shift has decreased cost, then we analyze the cost of shifting the service period by another period, i.e., shifting it to period $s-2$. We continue until cost increases and denote the resulting number of periods shifted to the left (to earlier periods) by $i_L^*(m,s)$, such that $i_L^*(m,s)$ is the largest positive integer such that $c(\tilde{\psi}(m,s,-i_L^*(m,s))) < c(\tilde{\psi}(m,s,-i_L^*(m,s)-1))$ (lines (4)-(10)). If $c(\tilde{\psi}(m,s,-1))$ is greater than $c(\psi)$, i.e., the shift to an earlier time period leads to a cost increase compared to the initial solution, then the best local shift to the left is equal to 1 time period ($i_L^*(m,s)=1$ (lines (1)- (3)).

Similarly, we analyze how shifts to the right (to later periods) affect cost and denote by $i_R^*(m,s)$ the smallest positive integer such that $c(\tilde{\psi}(m,s,i_R^*(m,s))) < c(\tilde{\psi}(m,s,i_R^*(m,s)+1))$, i.e., the number of periods to be shifted until an additional shift will result in higher cost (lines (16)-(20)). If $c(\tilde{\psi}(m,s,1))$ is greater than $c(\psi)$, i.e., if a shift to one later time period leads to a cost increase, then the best local shift to the right is equal to this shift ($i_R^*(m,s)=1$) (lines (11)-(12)).

After the determination of the best local shift to earlier and later time periods, the best local shift out of the two is determined. The best local shift $i^*(m,s)$ is $i^*(m,s) = -i_L^*(m,s)$, if $c(\tilde{\psi}(m,s,-i_L^*(m,s))) \leq c(\tilde{\psi}(m,s,i_R^*(m,s)))$ and $i^*(m,s) = i_R^*(m,s)$, otherwise (lines (21)-(25)). That means, if we compare the best local shift to earlier and to later periods, the best local shift is then the one with the highest cost savings. In case that both shifts lead to a cost increase compared to the initial solution, the one with the lowest cost decrease is the best local shift.

In total, the shifting module allows us to identify best local shifts as neighborhood solutions of an initial service table. Best local shifts may lead to cost savings as well as to an increase in cost. The module provides a helpful tool for the optimization heuristics in the following chapter to identify good service tables for the service routing problem.

7 Optimization Heuristics

In this chapter, we develop four heuristics to optimize the service routing problem based on the modules developed in Chapter 6. The approaches rely on the local and global search heuristics described in Chapter 4. The first two methods have the objective to find a local optimum of the service routing problem. The third and fourth approaches aim to escape from a local optimum to find a global optimum.

The first approach is a local random search algorithm that randomly chooses a shifting candidate and performs a best local shift by the shifting module in each iteration (Section 7.1.1). The second approach is a steepest descent approach (Section 7.1.2). In contrast to local random search, steepest descent explores all possible best local shifts before the service table is updated by the best found solution. Since both methods can get stuck in a local optimum, a third and fourth approach are developed to possibly find a global optimum. We introduce a simulated annealing approach that allows the local random search algorithm to accept cost increases to escape from a local optimum (Section 7.2.1). Then, we develop a method that enables the steepest descent approach to escape from the local optimum by a tabu search approach (Section 7.2.2). We will next describe the algorithms in detail.

7.1 Find Local Minimum

In the following, we describe two different approaches to find a local minimum for the service routing problem by adapting the ideas of local random search and steepest descent based on the remarks of Section 4.1. First, we explain the local random search approach. Then, we describe the deterministic approach of steepest descent.

N. Holtvogt, *The Service Routing Problem*, Edition KWV,
https://doi.org/10.1007/978-3-658-24126-1_7

7.1.1 Local Random Search

Under local random search (LRS), we consider best local shifts determined by the shifting module in random order. If a best local shift decreases cost, we update the service table and keep it otherwise. Figure 7.1 shows the flowchart of the algorithm. We start by choosing an initial solution. We adapt the approach of Jaillet et al. (2002)

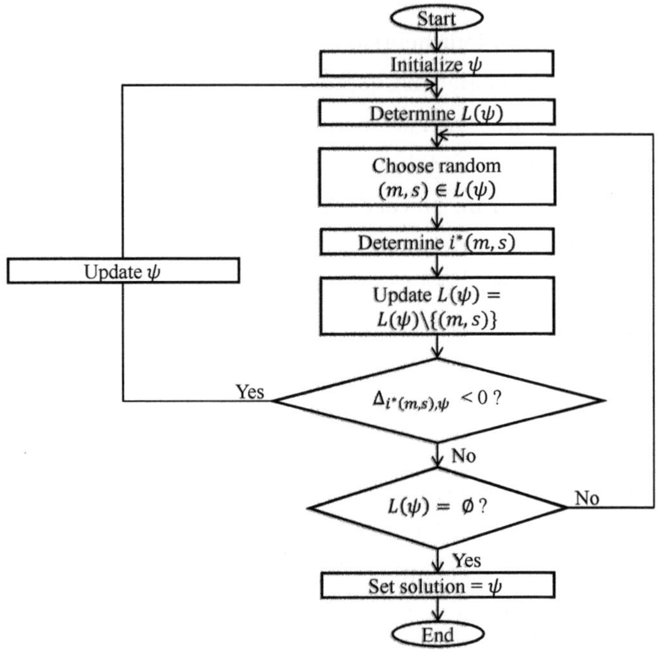

Figure 7.1: Local Random Search

and choose the latest starting time windows to generate the initial service table ψ. The resulting crew scheduling problem is solved optimally with the crew scheduling module and the resulting cost $c(\psi)$ becomes the benchmark solution to the service routing problem. Then, we determine the set of service period and site combinations $L(\psi)$ for table ψ. A random service period and site combination (m, s) is chosen and next, the best local shift $i^*(m, s)$ of this combination is determined.

If the resulting cost $c(\tilde{\psi}(m,s,i^*(m,s)))$ is less than the current minimum cost $c(\psi)$, i.e., $\Delta_{i^*(m,s),\psi} = c(\tilde{\psi}(m,s,i^*(m,s))) - c(\psi) < 0$, then the current service table ψ is updated. The service period and site combinations $L(\psi)$ of the updated service table ψ are determined and the process restarts by choosing a new random service period and site combination. If $\Delta_{i^*(m,s),\psi} > 0$ and not all service periods have been explored, i.e., $L(\psi) \neq \emptyset$, then a new random service period is chosen and the process starts again. If all service periods have been explored, the algorithm terminates with the current service table as the solution.

Figure 7.2 shows the example of the possible cost development during one optimization run until the local optimum is reached for an example with 18 sites and a required service after at most 3 days. This example gives us a first impression how the cost of the service routing problem can be decreased by local random search.

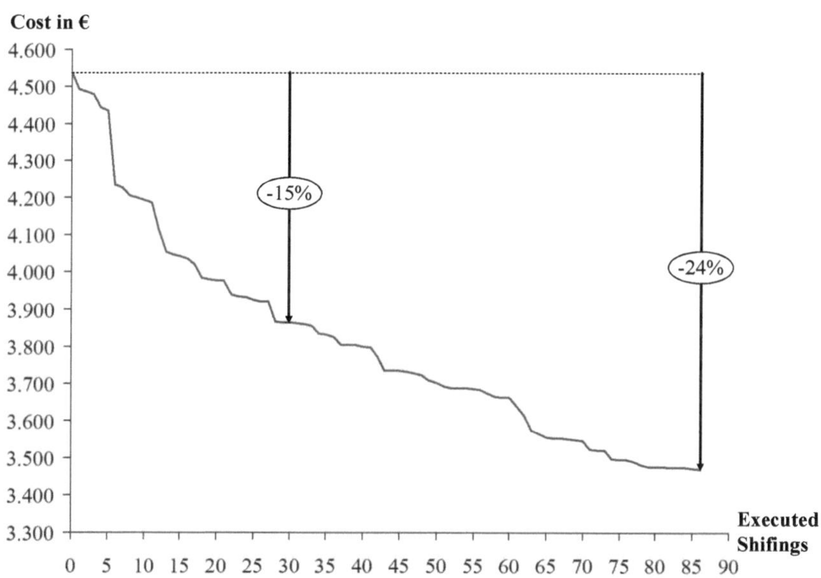

Figure 7.2: Example: Cost Development - Local Random Search

During the run, about 90 shiftings within a CPU time of about 300 sec have been executed until the local optimum with a cost decrease of about 24% is reached. The cost savings from one executed shifting to another vary a lot. However, high cost savings may already be realized by local random search after a third of the executed shiftings similar to this example.

7.1.2 Steepest Descent

The local random search algorithm is fast, but the random choice of the next service period and site combination adds randomness. In contrast to the local random search algorithm, the steepest descent (SD) algorithm is a deterministic approach. It explores all best local shifts of the service period and site combinations $L(\psi)$ before the service table is updated. Figure 7.3 shows the flowchart of the algorithm. Again,

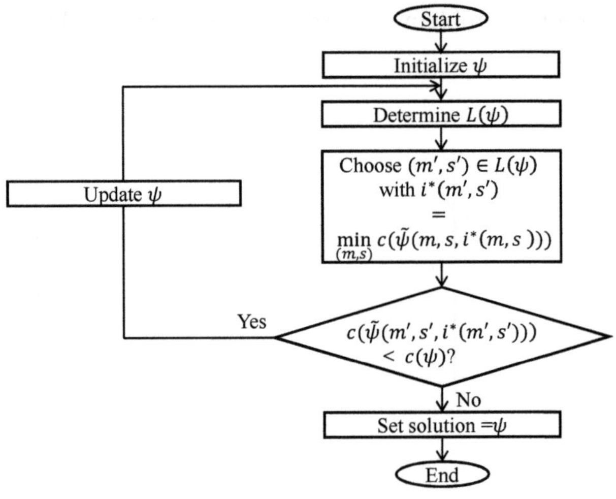

Figure 7.3: Steepest Descent

we choose the latest starting time windows to generate the initial service table ψ. For all service period and site combinations $L(\psi)$ of service table ψ, the shifting with the largest cost decrease $i^*(m', s') = \{i^*(m, s) | min_{(m,s)} c(\tilde{\psi}(m, s, i^*(m, s)))\}$ is chosen. If the cost $c(\tilde{\psi}(m', s', i^*(m', s')))\}$ is less than the cost of table ψ, the current best service table is updated by $\psi(m', s', i^*(m', s'))$. Then, all service periods $L(\psi)$ for the resulting

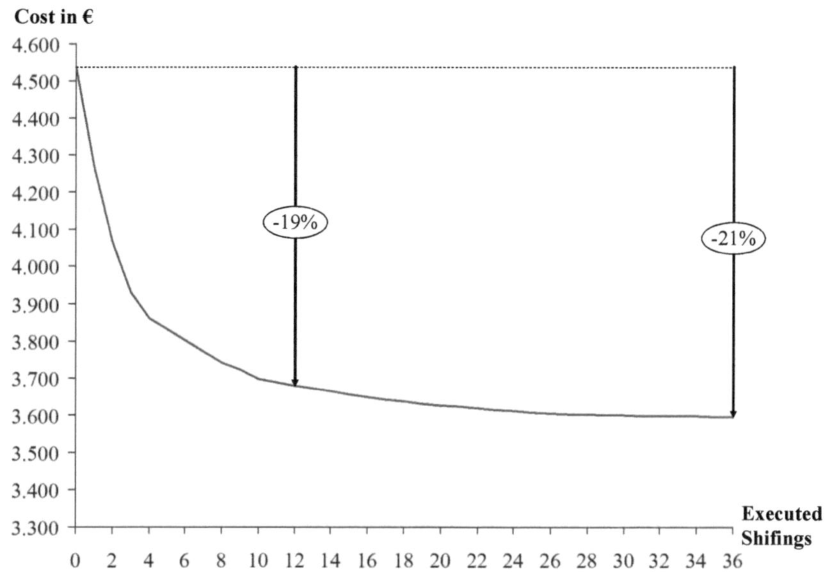

Figure 7.4: Example: Cost Development - Steepest Descent

service table are explored. This process is repeated until no more improvements can be found.

Also for steepest descent, we want to get an impression how the cost of the service routing problem can be decreased. Figure 7.4 shows the cost development during one optimization run of steepest descent for an example with 18 sites and a required service after at most 3 days.

During one steepest descent run, about 36 shiftings have been executed with a CPU time of about 377 seconds. As expected, this illustrates that it takes longer to execute a shifting compared to local random search. Local random search executes a shifting immediately and tabu search explores all best local shifts of the service period and site combinations before the service table is updated. In Figure 7.4, the local optimum is about 21%. During the run, the cost is decreasing with a declining rate and not varying like in Figure 7.2 for the example with local random search. Similar to the example for local random search, after a third of the executed shiftings are performed, high cost improvements have already been realized, i.e., after 12 executed shiftings, a cost decrease of about 19% is realized.

7.2 Global Search Heuristics for the Service Routing Problem

The local random search and steepest descent algorithms can get stuck in a local optimum. To escape a local optimum, simulated annealing or tabu search can be used (see Section 4.2). Our tests showed that the combination of the local random search approach with simulated annealing and the steepest descent approach with tabu search lead to good solutions to escape from a local optimum.

7.2.1 Simulated Annealing

The local random search algorithm terminates when no improvements can be found. Often, the solution is not a global optimum of the service routing problem. We adapt the simulated annealing (SA) approach of Kirkpatrick et al. (1983) to escape from local optima by occasionally accepting solutions that worsen the objective function value.

Figure 7.5 shows the flowchart of the algorithm. Simulated annealing starts with the service table $\psi \in \Psi$ of the local optimum determined by local random search and the corresponding cost $c(\psi)$. A random service period and site combination (m, s) of the service table is chosen and the best local shift with cost $c(i^*(m, s))$ and the difference $\Delta_{i^*(m,s),\psi} = c(\tilde{\psi}(m, s, i^*(m, s))) - c(\psi)$ are determined. If $\Delta_{i^*(m,s),\psi} < 0$, the resulting service table is accepted. Otherwise it is only accepted with probability $P(\Delta_{i^*(m,s),\psi}, T) = \exp^{-\frac{\Delta_{i^*(m,s),\psi}}{T}}$, where T is the temperature (see Section 4.2.1). In the next iteration, the temperature is decreased and a new random service period is chosen. The process is repeated until a predetermined CPU time t_{SA} has elapsed. The service table that resulted in the crew schedule with the best solution among all considered tables marks the solution of the algorithm.

Simulated annealing requires a reasonable determination of the starting temperature T_0 and the cooling rate cr. In our approach, the two parameters will be determined based on given acceptance probabilities for the beginning and the end of the run time. If we start with a very high temperature and decrease the temperature very

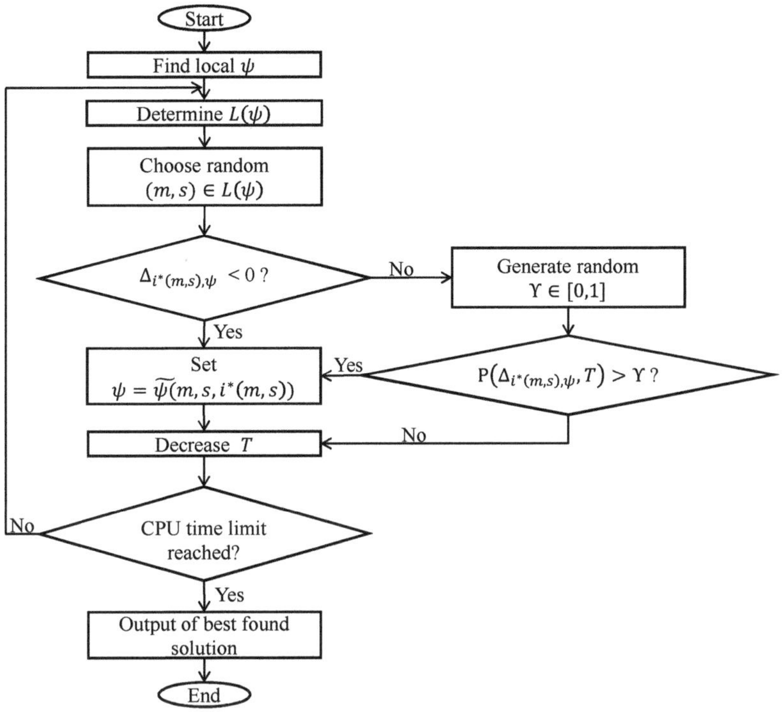

Figure 7.5: Simulated Annealing

slowly, simulated annealing can find the global optimum, but run times become excessive. The parameter must be chosen reasonable to find a good trade-off between solution quality and run time. We set $T_{it} = cr\,T_{it-1}$, whereas cr describes the cooling rate and it the number of the current iteration.

For our approach, we base the determination of the starting temperature T_0 and the cooling rate cr on the CPU limit t_{SA} and define acceptance probabilities for the beginning and the end of a simulated annealing run. At the beginning, after n_0 iterations, an acceptance probability of p_0 should be reached. And at the end, after n_{SA} iterations, an acceptance probability of p_E is desired (Figure 7.6). First, we perform the local random search approach to find the local optimum. The corresponding CPU time is denoted by t_0. Additionally, we count the number of iterations n_0 needed to determine the optimal cost of all explored service tables during the local random search run. Based on the predetermined CPU time t_{SA} of the total run time of the algorithm, the number of iterations n_{SA} for determining T_0 and cr results in an estimated number of iterations $n_{SA} = \frac{n_0}{t_0} t_{SA}$.

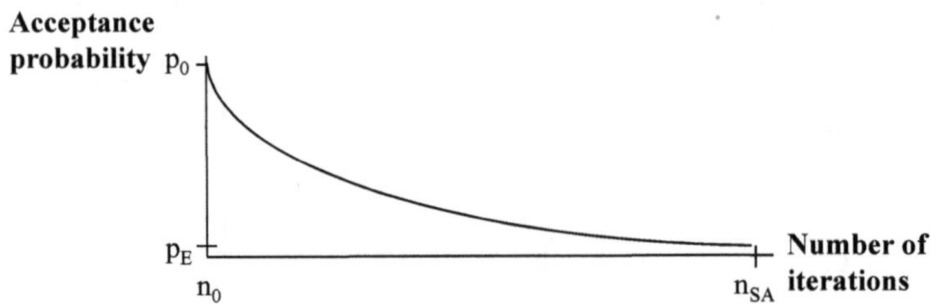

Figure 7.6: Temperature - Simulated Annealing

Based on n_{SA} and given acceptance probabilities for the beginning p_0 and for the end p_E, T_0 and cr can be determined. We consider the average of all higher cost of best local shifts, that do not result in an improvement of the current solution, as a benchmark cost factor c_b. Then, c_b is compared to the cost $c(\psi)$ of the local optimum. We choose the parameters such that $p_0 = \exp^{-\frac{c_b - c(\psi)}{T_0}}$. For given p_0, the starting temperature T_0 is determined as follows:

$$p_0 = \exp^{-\frac{c_b - c(\psi)}{T_0}} \tag{7.1}$$

$$\Leftrightarrow \log(p_0) = -\frac{c_b - c(\psi)}{T_0} \tag{7.2}$$

$$\Leftrightarrow \quad T_0 = -\frac{(c_b - c(\psi))}{\log(p_0)}. \tag{7.3}$$

After the estimated iterations n_{SA}, an acceptance probability of $p_E = \exp^{-\frac{c_b - c(\psi)}{T_E}}$ should be reached, whereas T_E is the temperature at the end of the period. With $T_E = T_0 cr^{n_{SA}}$ and Equation (7.3), the cooling rate cr is determined as follows:

$$p_E = \exp^{-\frac{c_b - c(\psi)}{T_E}} \quad (7.4)$$
$$\Leftrightarrow T_E = -\frac{(c_b - c(\psi))}{\log(p_E)} \quad (7.5)$$
$$\Leftrightarrow T_0 cr^{n_{SA}} = -\frac{(c_b - c(\psi))}{\log(p_E)} \quad (7.6)$$
$$\Leftrightarrow cr = \left(\frac{log(p_0)}{log(p_E)}\right)^{\frac{1}{n_{SA}}}. \quad (7.7)$$

Figure 7.7 gives us an impression of the possible cost development during one optimization run of simulated annealing for an example with 18 sites and a required service after at most 3 days. The CPU time limit was set to 1746 sec and about 550

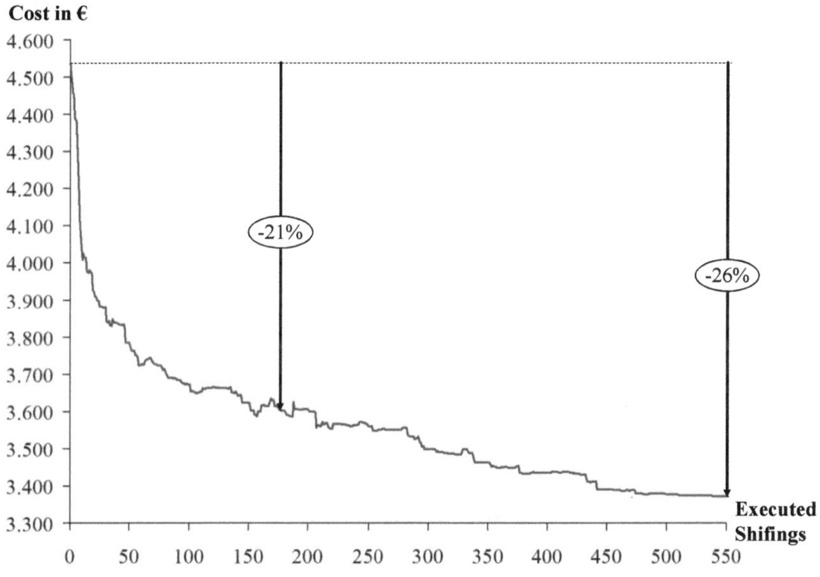

Figure 7.7: Example: Cost Development - Simulated Annealing

shiftings have been executed. The cost decreases from one executed shifting to another vary a lot. For this specific run, after a third of all executed shiftings, a high cost decrease of 21% is realized. The best found solution leads to a cost saving of about 26%.

7.2.2 Tabu Search

After a local optimum has been found by steepest descent, all service period and site combinations $L(\psi)$ of the local optimal setting ψ are again explored. We choose the best local shift that results in the smallest cost increase compared to the current optimal solution. This approach can lead to cyclic solutions, i.e., if we choose the service table $\psi' \in \Psi$ with higher cost in case of the predecessor setting $\psi \in \Psi$, it is possible that again table $\psi \in \Psi$ is chosen in the next iteration. To avoid these cyclic solutions, the tabu search (TS) approach of Glover (1990) is applied and modified to suit the structure of the discussed problem.

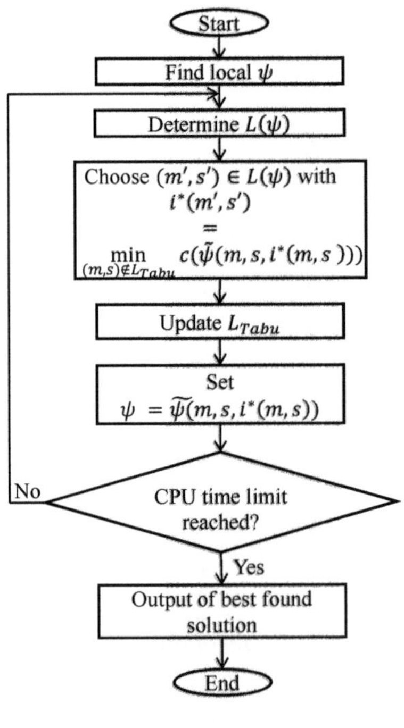

Figure 7.8: Tabu Search

Figure 7.8 shows the flowchart of the algorithm. After a service table with higher cost is accepted, the corresponding service period (m, s') is marked on a tabu list L_{Tabu} for a predetermined number of iterations, so that the service delivery will not be shifted again for that time. Thus, the direct shifting of service period (m, s') is forbidden. We also prohibit the indirect shifting of (m, s'), i.e., the shifting of a service period that leads to a shifting of (m, s') is also not allowed. After updating L_{Tabu}, the service table ψ is replaced by the last accepted service table and the process restarts. The approach terminates after a predetermined CPU time and the service table that resulted in the crew schedule with the best solution marks the solution of the algorithm.

Figure 7.9 gives us an impression of the possible cost development during one optimization run of tabu search for an example with 18 sites and a required service after at most 3 days.

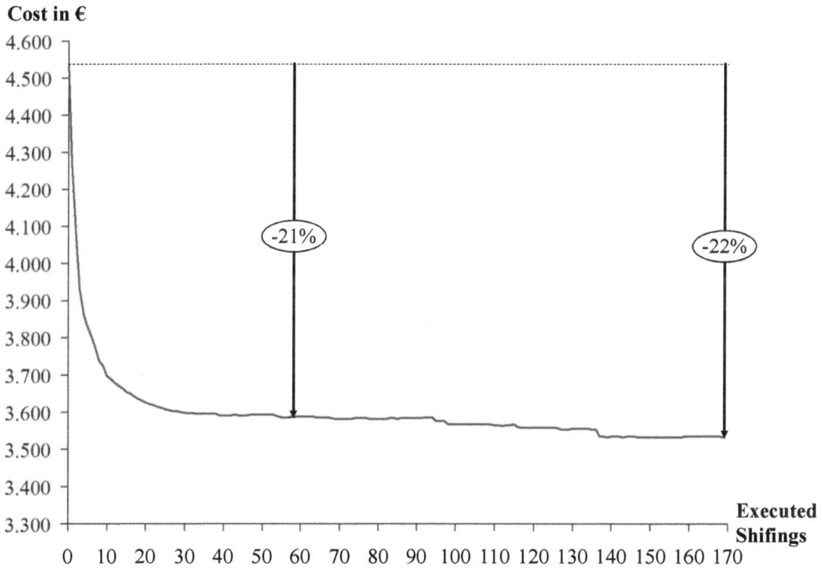

Figure 7.9: Example: Cost Development - Tabu Search

During a run time of 1764 sec, 170 shiftings have been executed. Due to the acceptance of cost increases during on tabu search run, the cost line is not strictly decreasing. Similar to the examples of the other approaches, the highest cost increase is realized after the execution of the first shiftings.

8 Computational Results

We test the performance of our approaches based on four test scenarios with different numbers of sites and demand densities. The algorithms are coded in C++ and LPs are solved by IBM CPLEX 12.1. The network algorithm is based on the Boost Graph library (Siek et al. (2002)), Boost version 1.43.0. All numerical tests were performed on a 64-bit Windows 7 system with a 2.4 GHz Intel Dual Core T7700 Processor and 4.0 GB RAM.

This chapter is structured as follows: The test scenarios are introduced in Section 8.1. Then, we describe the parameterization of the solution approach in Section 8.2 and finally, evaluate their performances (Section 8.3) and the sensitivity of the performance (Section 8.4).

8.1 Test Scenarios

The scenarios differ in the number of sites and in demand densities. Based on the network structure that motivated our research, the test scenarios consist of 9 and 18 sites. The sites are geographically distributed over the mid-west of Germany. Fig-

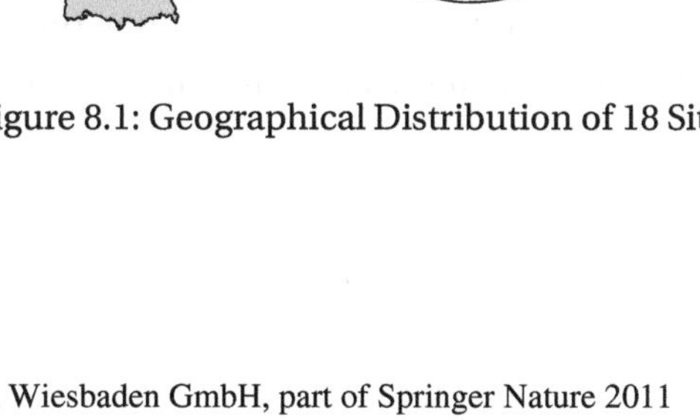

Figure 8.1: Geographical Distribution of 18 Sites

N. Holtvogt, *The Service Routing Problem*, Edition KWV,
https://doi.org/10.1007/978-3-658-24126-1_8

ure 8.1 shows an example with 18 sites.

We analyze different demand densities. Under low demand density, a service is required at each site after at most 6 days. Under high demand density, service is required after at most 3 days. Figure 8.2 gives an overview of the four resulting test scenarios.

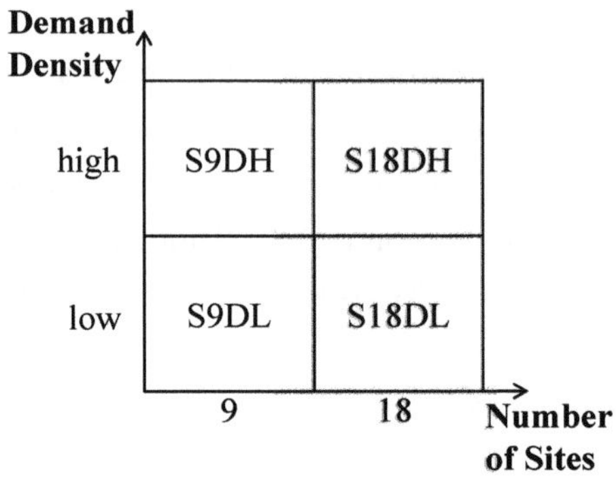

Figure 8.2: Test Scenarios

In our example, sites are opened from 8:00 to 20:00 and demand occurs only during this time interval. Service must be provided during opening hours. The service time is $sd = 15$ minutes and each day is divided into 48 time periods/day. A complete enumeration of all possible service tables would include a service table with a service in each period. For 18 sites, one has 19 options for each period: One can choose no service or a service at one of the 18 sites. The maximum duty length is given by the maximum work time of 8 hours or 32 periods. Therefore, there are more than 19^{32} different service duties per day that have to be examined. This means that there exists at least 10^{40} possible service duty combinations/day. That demonstrates the complexity of the problem instances.

All computational results of this chapter are based on labor cost of 8.15 €/h and travel cost of 0.30 €/km. We will solve the service routing problem over a planning horizon of 14 days. This planning horizon is commonly used for a rolling-horizon framework, i.e., only the first week is actually implemented, but this week is influenced by the second week to consider the future (Campbell and Savelsbergh (2004)).

8.2 Parameterization of Solution Approaches

The simulated annealing and tabu search algorithms require parameterization. In this subsection, we describe how we determine appropriate parameter values for both algorithms.

8.2.1 Simulated Annealing

Simulated annealing requires the specification of a starting temperature T_0, a cooling rate cr, and a CPU time limit as stopping criterion for the approach.

We determine the starting temperature and the cooling rate based on acceptance probabilities at the beginning and the end of the run with Equations (7.3) and (7.7) (see Section 7.2.1). To identify good acceptance probabilities, we performed multiple test runs with different combinations of starting and ending acceptance probabilities p_0 and p_E. A starting acceptance probability of $p_0 = 80\%$ and an ending acceptance probability of $p_E = 20\%$ provided consistently good results and we use these parameters in our experiments.

For the CPU time limit, we also need an appropriate parameterization. Local random search is the basis for our simulated annealing approach, because it provides the initial solution. Therefore, we will apply a multiple of the average CPU time of a local random search run. The quality of the solution is (non-strictly) increasing in CPU time. Thus, a trade-off decision must be made between CPU time and solution quality. To make this decision, we analyzed how the cost of a solution depends on the CPU time. We denote the ratio between the CPU time of a simulated annealing run and the average CPU time of a local random search run by mk. A mk-ratio of 5, for instance, corresponds to a CPU time of simulated annealing that is 5 times higher than the average CPU time of local random search. Our tests indicated that a mk-ratio of 6 provides a good trade-off between CPU time and quality. We use this ratio in our experiments.

8.2.2 Tabu Search

Tabu search asks for a good tabu list management. In this thesis, we chose a static and strict tabu list (see Section 7.2.2) to limit the number of required parameterizations. This tabu list stores the blocked service period and site combinations for a certain number of iterations, the number of blocked shiftings (NBS). We analyzed the performance of tabu search for different values of NBS in multiple test runs. The results indicated that a good NBS is 10 for 9 sites and 30 for a scenario with 18 sites. We use these values in our experiments.

8.3 Performance Evaluation

We next evaluate the performance of the heuristics. First, we analyze the graph characteristics and provide some details on the implementation. Then, we evaluate the performance of the crew scheduling module. Finally, we report computational results for local random search, steepest descent, simulated annealing, and tabu search.

8.3.1 Size of Graph

In Section 6.1, we developed a crew scheduling module to optimize service crew scheduling problems. In the following, we want to evaluate the complexity of solving multiple crew scheduling problems during a run of an optimization heuristic. We use the same procedures for generating graphs and solving the crew scheduling problem in all heuristics. The numerical results are based on the steepest descent heuristic, but the general insights are the same for the other heuristics. During one steepest descent run, multiple service tables and consequently multiple service crew scheduling problems are explored. Each service crew scheduling problem is modeled as a connection network in a graph. For the test scenarios, we evaluate the average number of nodes and arcs of the crew scheduling problems. We also determine the average number of subproblem executions. Furthermore, we analyze how many shiftings are analyzed and actually executed during one optimization run. Table 8.1 shows that the average number of nodes, arcs and the subproblem executions is increasing over-proportionally in the problem size.

In the shifting module of the heuristics, we may generate service tables that have already been generated previously. To avoid the recalculation of the optimal crew schedule, we check that a service table has not been considered before we start the crew scheduling module. In the optimization, we take advantage of the large number of redundant service tables and apply the crew scheduling module only once to each unique service table. Hence, the number of generated columns can be reduced significantly. We denote the reduced number of columns as *unique columns*. Table 8.1 shows the average total number of columns (Row *Total # of Columns Generated*) and the average number of unique columns (Row *Total # of Unique Columns*) and highlights the importance of determining unique columns only.

	S9DL	S9DH	S18DL	S18DH
Avg # of Nodes	9,16	13,91	13,93	24,52
Avg # of Arcs	21,17	48,29	47,96	147,78
Avg # of Subproblem Executions	2,96	3,02	3,30	3,50
Total # of Columns Generated	632.864	4.983.582	9.043.039	137.532.898
Total # of Unique Columns	14.091	171.005	202.357	3.632.613
Total # of Shiftings Analysed	4.880	6.911	12.270	24.746
Total # of Shiftings Executed	29	18	35	36

Table 8.1: Performance Indicators of Steepest Descent Algorithm

The table illustrates that the check for unique service tables significantly reduces the number of columns generated. For instance, for test scenario S18DH the number of generated columns can be reduced by 97.4% from 137.5 million to 3.6 million.

8.3.2 Performance of Crew Scheduling Module

In the following, we want to evaluate the average performance of our crew scheduling module. The optimal service schedule for a given service table is determined by the module. To analyze the performance of the crew scheduling module for all four heuristics, Table 8.2 shows the average time to find the optimal service schedule for a given service table during one steepest descent run. The general insights are the same for all heuristics.

Generally, the table illustrates that the total CPU time to solve a certain service table is over-proportionally increasing in demand density. Furthermore, for large problem

	S9DL				S9DH			
Solution Approach	LRS	SD	SA	TS	LRS	SD	SA	TS
Average CPU total (incl. Overhead)	3.80	1.76	3.55	10.11	4.72	5.88	7.61	8.68
Average CPU Graph Generation	2.32	1.21	1.22	1.54	1.99	2.98	2.59	1.99
Subproblem								
Average CPU Lower Bound	0.47	0.17	1.43	6.43	1.53	1.97	3.16	4.74
Average CPU Upper Bound	<0.01	<0.01	<0.01	0.03	<0.01	<0.01	<0.01	<0.01
Average CPU Branch and Price	<0.01	<0.01	0.02	0.17	0.02	<0.01	0.04	0.01
Master Problem								
Average CPU Lower Bound	0.61	0.38	0.54	1.35	0.70	0.91	1.09	1.32
Average CPU Upper Bound	<0.01	<0.01	<0.01	<0.01	<0.01	<0,01	<0.01	<0.01
Average CPU Branch and Price	0.01	<0.01	0.02	0.09	0.02	0.02	0.06	0.03

	S18DL				S18DH			
Solution Approach	LRS	SD	SA	TS	LRS	SD	SA	TS
Average CPU total (incl. Overhead)	6.18	1.79	11.26	7.59	44.99	14.17	113.64	70.31
Average CPU Graph Generation	2.22	1.44	2.18	2.33	2.43	1.30	2.51	1.49
Subproblem								
Average CPU Lower Bound	1.86	1.09	6.41	2.82	31.10	11.22	90.78	51.48
Average CPU Upper Bound	0.02	0.01	0.02	0.04	0.39	0.09	1.01	1.23
Average CPU Branch and Price	0.10	0.08	0.12	0.08	2.10	0.43	5.63	5.95
Master Problem								
Average CPU Lower Bound	0.80	0.52	1.48	0.96	4.68	2.12	8.52	5.52
Average CPU Upper Bound	<0.01	<0.01	<0.01	0.01	0.04	0.03	0.06	0.07
Average CPU Branch and Price	0.15	0.10	0.10	0.21	0.81	0.29	1.07	1.07

Table 8.2: Branch-and-Price: Average CPU Time (in ms)

instances, the main computational effort is in the subproblem in the determination of the lower bound, i.e., the solution of the LP-relaxation. The computational effort for the determination of an integer solution in the master problem by branch-and-price is also increasing in problem size, but compared to the one of the lower bound it is relatively small for the problem instances considered.

8.3.3 Performance of Solution Approaches

In Chapter 7, we developed four different solution approaches: local random search, steepest descent, simulated annealing, and tabu search. To evaluate the performance of these approaches, we compare the cost of the solutions with the cost of a benchmark solution (BS). The benchmark solution results from the behavior of the service providing company that motivated our research. Currently, the company does not take the shifting of services into account. Therefore, to determine the benchmark solution, we assume that all services start at the latest service times, i.e., that no services are advanced and compute the optimal solution for this table. Note that this solution minimizes the number of services, but not necessarily total cost.

Local random search and simulated annealing contain stochastic elements and the results of two optimizations generally differ. Therefore, we perform multiple runs and report the averages. We choose 180 local random search runs to get a good choice of different randomly generated results. For simulated annealing, we use a CPU time limit of 6 times the time of a local random search run. To compare the performance of local random search and simulated annealing for given CPU time budgets, we compare the best solutions found in 6 local random search runs with that of a single simulated annealing run (see Section 8.2.1). Consequently, we perform $\frac{180}{6} = 30$ simulated annealing runs.

Table 8.3 reports the results for the four test scenarios. Row *Avg Cost* reports the average cost of the solution, row *Cost of BS* the cost of the benchmark solution. Row *Cost of BS* contains the cost saving the algorithms achieve over the benchmark solution. Row *Minimum Cost* shows the cost of the best solution found in any runs. The table shows that the CPU time increases in the problem size and demand den-

	S9DL				S9DH			
Solution Approach	LRS	SD	SA	TS	LRS	SD	SA	TS
Total CPU Time in sec	174	31	174	174	216	106	216	216
Avg Cost	1187.21	1219.18	1217.79	1106.80	2001.79	2009.97	1996.30	1952.87
Cost of BS	1465.06	1465.06	1465.06	1465.06	2511.73	2511.73	2511.73	2511.73
Cost Savings	18.97%	16.78%	16.88%	24.45%	20.30%	19.98%	20.52%	22.25%
Minimum Cost	1106.80	1106.80	1106.80	1106.80	1913.80	1913.80	1913.80	1913.80

	S18DL				S18DH			
Solution Approach	LRS	SD	SA	TS	LRS	SD	SA	TS
Total CPU Time in sec	372	128	372	372	1764	377	1764	1764
Avg Cost	2220.07	2242.62	2249.54	2241.91	3548.00	3595.74	3584.82	3532.21
Cost of BS	2734.33	2734.33	2734.33	2734.33	4537.19	4537.19	4537.19	4537.19
Cost Savings	18.81%	17.98%	17.73%	18.01%	21.80%	20.75%	20.99%	22.15%
Minimum Cost	2156.26	2156.26	2156.26	2156.26	3371.68	3371.68	3371.68	3371.68

Table 8.3: Performance of Solution Approaches

sity. However, even for the large problem with 18 sites and high demand density, the problem can be solved within 30 minutes. Depending on the problem and the solution approach, the cost improvements of the heuristics over the benchmark solution range between 16.78% and 22.25%. The results show that taking advantage of the option to advance services is highly beneficial. By moving some service deliveries to earlier times than the latest starting times, great savings can be obtained. Out of the four heuristics analyzed, the tabu search heuristic seems to achieve the best results. For three of the four problems, it found the best solution.

To get a better understanding on how these savings are generated, we analyze the problem with 9 sites and high density demand in detail (Tables 8.4 and 8.5).

	Benchmark Solution				
	# of Service Duties	Avg Cost of Duty	Avg # of Services/Duty	Avg Work Time (w/oTravel) in Min	Avg Travel Time in Min
Day					
1	3	59,2	1,7	25	45,3
2	2	90,1	2,5	37,5	94,5
3	2	80,9	3	45	83,5
4	2	69,3	2	30	62,5
5	3	71	2	30	68
6	2	77,3	2,5	37,5	73,5
7	2	66,4	2	30	59,5
8	3	76,5	2,3	35	78,3
9	3	62,2	1,7	25	47
10	3	75	2	25	71,7
11	2	77,7	2,5	37,5	77
12	3	68,5	1,7	25	62
13	3	75,6	2	30	74,3
14	2	62,2	2	30	50
Avg	2,50	72,3	2,1	31,6	67,7

Table 8.4: Service Duties - Benchmark Solution

The benchmark solution requires 72 visits during a 14 days period and the tabu search solution uses 86 visits. However, the visits of the tabu search solution are arranged such that total cost is reduced. For instance, the number of service duties for tabu search is reduced from an average of 2.5 to 1.57 service duties per day. Furthermore, the number of services per duty is increased from an average of 2.13 to 4.18 deliveries per service duty. The average duty time is about 99 minutes for the benchmark solution and 167 minutes for the tabu search solution. Since a minimum work time of $w_{min} = 5$ hours/day $= 300$ minutes/day have to be paid, the service duties of

	Tabu Search				
	# of Service Duties	Avg Cost of Duty	Avg # of Services/Duty	Avg Work Time (w/o Travel) in Min	Avg Travel Time in Min
Day					
1	2	67,8	5,5	82,5	63
2	1	116,5	9	135	149
3	2	96,0	4	60	106
4	1	95,7	3	45	97
5	1	139	6	90	161
6	1	147,3	6	90	185
7	1	66,9	3	45	62
8	2	85,4	4,0	60	89
9	1	96,3	4,0	60	87
10	2	87,6	2,5	37,5	99,5
11	2	83,2	3	45	89,5
12	2	75,0	2,5	37,5	74
13	2	90,0	2,5	37,5	100,0
14	2	84,1	3,5	52,5	98
Avg	1,57	95,0	4,2	62,7	104,3

Table 8.5: Service Duties - Tabu Search

the tabu search solution are much more profitable.

Figures 8.3 and 8.4 show the optimized schedules for day 5 for the benchmark and the tabu search solutions. The benchmark solution consists of 6 service deliveries per day (Figure 8.3). Due to the constraints, the deliveries must be covered by 3 duties. The service table of the tabu search approach consists also of 6 service deliveries for day 5 (Figure 8.4). However, the services at site 3 as well as at site 5 are advanced and the service of site 4 is postponed. That results in only 1 service duty that can cover all 6 service deliveries within the maximum work time. Consequently, the cost for day 5 are reduced in this example from 213.04 € to 138.75 €.

Benchmark Solution:

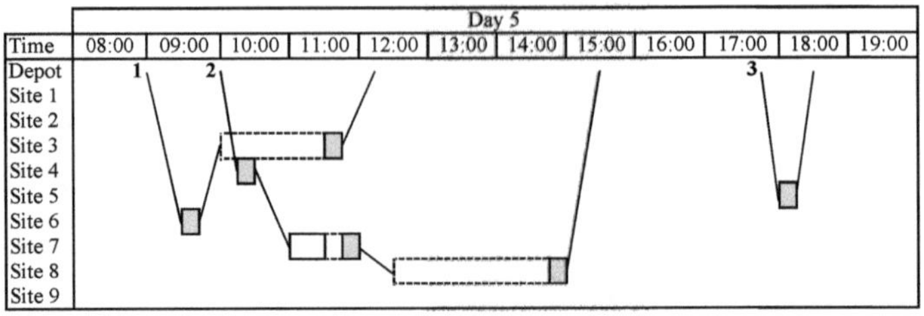

Figure 8.3: Schedule - Benchmark Solution

Tabu Search:

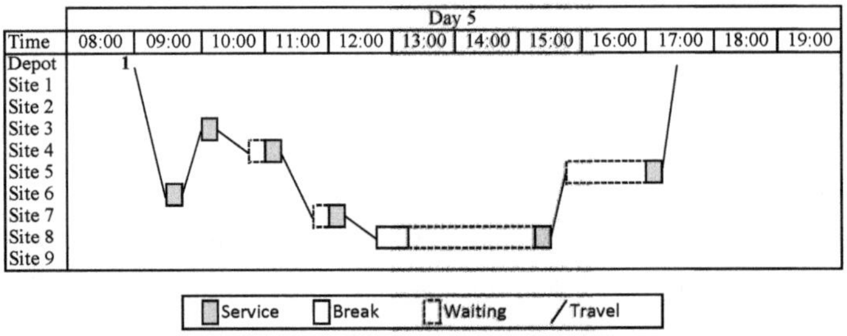

Figure 8.4: Schedule - Tabu Search

8.4 Sensitivity of Performance

We next analyze the effect of demand densities, maximum and minimum work times on the solution performance. We use tabu search to solve the problems, because Section 8.3.3 showed that the heuristic is the best one for our test scenarios.

8.4.1 Demand Density

We use configurations with very low, low, high, and very high demand densities for our test scenarios with 9 and 18 sites.

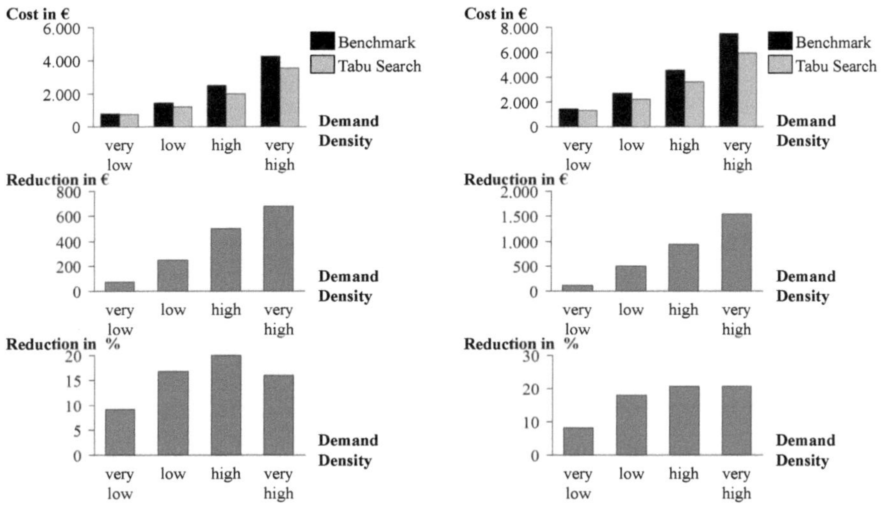

(a) 9 Sites (b) 18 Sites

Figure 8.5: Sensitivity of Performance depending on Demand Density

The low and high configurations correspond to those used above. In the very low demand density schedule, we use half the demand density of the low demand density schedule, i.e., service is required after at most 12 days. In the very high demand density setting, we use twice the demand density of the high demand density setting, i.e., service is required after at most 1.5 days.

Figure 8.5 illustrates the effect of the demand densities on the solution. The results show that the absolute savings of the optimized solutions are increasing in the demand density. The relative savings range between 8% and 21%. For very low demand densities, the relative savings are moderate, because the potential set of services that can be combined is small. As the demand density increases, the set of services that can potentially be combined increases and the optimization takes advantage of this by advancing services. However, if the demand density increases above a certain threshold, the relative savings are decreasing (or at least not increasing anymore), because an increasing demand density leads to an increasing number of service periods. A high demand density leads to a small maximum distance dis_m between services at a site m (Section 5.2.4). Therefore, there are only a few possibilities to shift service deliveries to achieve a service table that is feasible and reduces the overall cost.

8.4.2 Maximum Work Time

We analyze the effect of the length of the maximum work time on test scenarios S9DH and S18DH. We use configurations with a maximum work time of 6, 7, 8, 9, and 10 hours. The minimum work time is equal to 5 hours. Figure 8.6 shows the results.

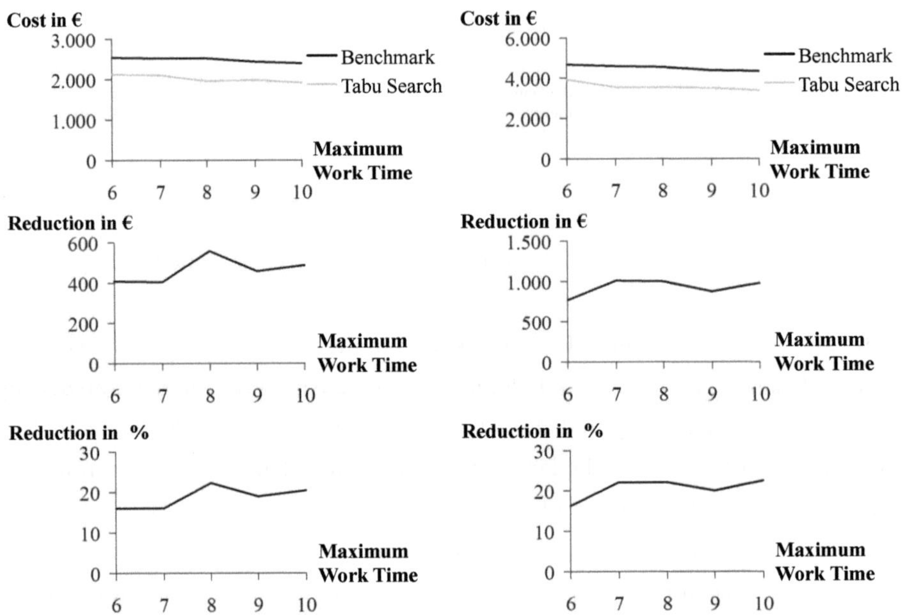

(a) S9DH (b) S18DH

Figure 8.6: Sensitivity of Performance depending on Maximum Work Time

It illustrates that the benchmark solution and the tabu search solution are slowly decreasing with increasing maximum work time. The results show that the maximum work time has a small effect on the cost of the solution and that relaxations of labor law that asks for a maximum work time of 8 hours would not reduce cost considerably in the examples we analyzed.

The effect that the cost for increasing maximum work time does not have a big impact on the solutions is explained by the average duty work time. In Figure 8.7, the average duty time is slowly increasing with increasing maximum working time, but for both considered scenarios a long maximum work time is not profitable.

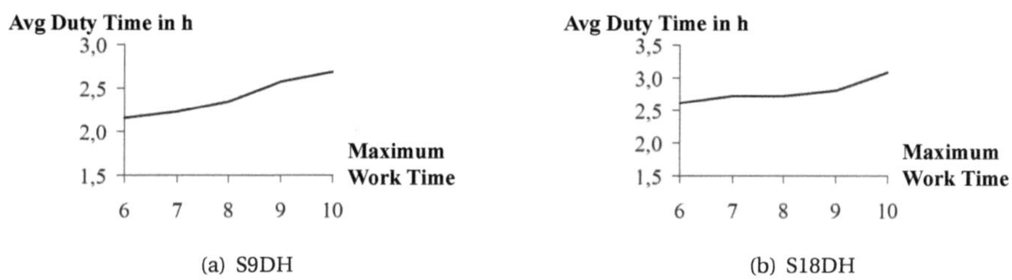

Figure 8.7: Average Service Duty Time

8.4.3 Minimum Work Time

We also analyze the effect of the length of the minimum work time on test scenarios S9DH and S18DH. We use configurations with a minimum work time of $0, 1, ..., 6$ hours. The maximum work time is equal to 8 hours. Figure 8.8 shows the results.

The figure shows that the cost of the benchmark solution and the tabu search solution are increasing in minimum work time. The example shows, that the application of a shifting approach is very important, if a minimum work time has to be paid.

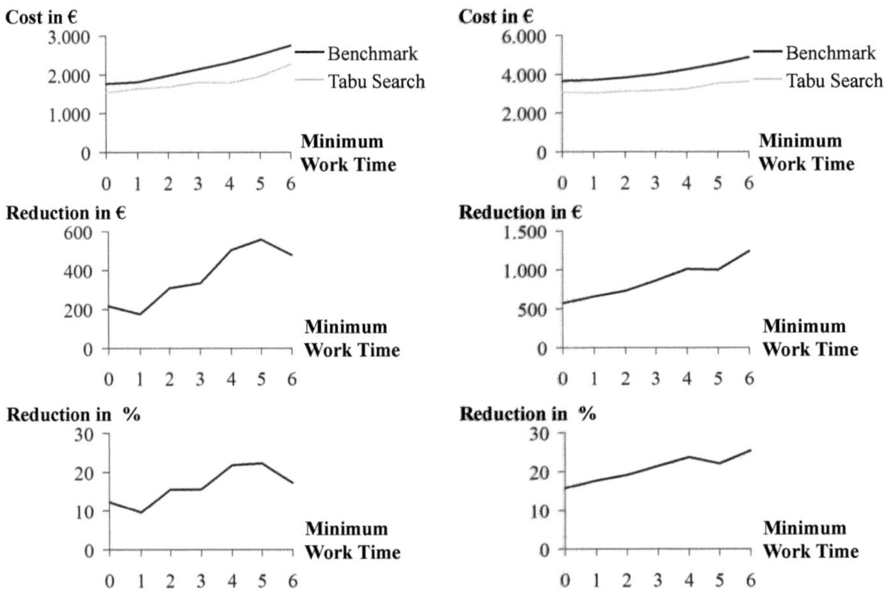

(a) S9DH (b) S18DH

Figure 8.8: Sensitivity of Performance depending on Minimum Work Time

9 Closing Remarks and Outlook

In this thesis, we introduced the service routing problem and developed appropriate solution approaches. The objective was the determination of a service table that minimizes total cost and obeys a set of work time regulations. In a straightforward solution, which we referred to as the benchmark solution, all services take place at the latest service times. Hence, the number of services is minimized, but the possibility of shifting service times is neglected. In an optimal solution, a trade-off decision between the number of services and the shifting of service times must be made to minimize the cost of a service crew schedule. Because of the high complexity of the service routing problem, optimal solution approaches result in excessive run times and we relied on heuristics. Our general approach was to efficiently explore multiple neighborhood solutions to quickly find solutions with large improvements relative to the benchmark solution.

The thesis was structured in seven main chapters. In the following, we summarize the main points of each chapter.

In **Chapter 2**, we gave a comprehensive overview of different routing and scheduling problems and reviewed several solution approaches. The service routing problem belongs to this class of problems and we wanted to identify suitable solution methods. Concerning the routing problem, we described the traveling salesman problem, the vehicle routing problem and the vehicle routing problem with time windows. As a result, we identified metaheuristics that enabled us to explore multiple neighborhood solutions efficiently. For the service routing problem, multiple different service tables exist. An exact evaluation of all feasible tables may lead to high computational effort. Therefore, we focused on local and global search heuristics due to their simplicity and flexibility to solve large problem instances. We described the crew scheduling problem to find solution approaches for the service routing problem with fixed delivery

N. Holtvogt, *The Service Routing Problem*, Edition KWV,
https://doi.org/10.1007/978-3-658-24126-1_9

times. Branch-and-price was identified as an efficient method to solve service tables to optimality. Finally, we explained the inventory routing problem: a combination of routing and inventory decisions. The problem has some similarities to the service routing problem, because it includes the influence on delivery times and optionally multiple deliveries per location. Although we saw that the inventory problem faces other challenges than the service routing problem, e.g., vehicle load and inventory capacities, and less focus on work time regulations, we identified a good first approach of decomposing the service routing problem into two subproblems.

In **Chapter 3**, we presented the fundamentals of column generation and branch-and-price to solve crew scheduling problems optimally. We illustrated the approaches to provide a comprehensive theoretical foundation to solve service tables optimally in the subsequent chapters. The chapter showed the decisions and challenges to be made for our solution approaches, like the decisions on modeling the master problem and the subproblem, and the challenges on finding service duties and integer solutions efficiently.

In **Chapter 4**, we adapted local and global search heuristics identified in Chapter 2 to explore different service tables efficiently to find (local) optima. We gave a detailed description of local random search, steepest descent, simulated annealing, and tabu search approaches due to their flexibility and simplicity. The chapter provided a useful foundation for the development of solution approaches for the service routing problem. This enabled us to decide on how to move from one service table to another service table and when to terminate the exploration of neighborhood solutions.

In **Chapter 5**, we described the service routing problem after the fundamental basics were clarified in Chapters 2 - 4. We detailed the problem specifications and highlighted the importance of exploring different service tables to decrease crew scheduling cost. The chapter prepared us for the development of suitable solution approaches.

In **Chapter 6**, we introduced two important parts of our solution approaches. We first decomposed the service routing problem into a service crew scheduling problem and a shifting problem. Then, we developed a crew scheduling module and a shifting module to solve the respective problem. The crew scheduling module solves a service table optimally. We adapted branch-and-price to the requirements of the crew scheduling problem, e.g., network requirements. To keep memory requirements and computational time at a low level, we developed efficient and quick procedures, e.g., for the labeling and duty selection process. To find an optimal integer solution, we chose a helpful upper bound by adapting the variable fixing of Grönkvist (2005) and customized the branching rule of Foster and Ryan (1981). Furthermore, we implemented an efficient node and arc construction algorithm and excluded infeasible connections already in the construction process. The shifting module introduced the new idea of a local shift. Based on this idea, we developed a greedy algorithm to determine a best local shift that results in a new service table. The best local shift approach was a good basis for the solution approaches of the subsequent chapter that aim to explore multiple service tables.

In **Chapter 7**, we combined the modules developed in Chapter 6 to efficient local and global search heuristics relying on the approaches described in Chapter 4. The four resulting solution approaches enabled us to decide which service tables to explore and when to terminate the search process.

In **Chapter 8**, we applied the solution approaches to different test scenarios. We illustrated the high potential of decreasing cost by shifting service times. For a benchmark solution, the services in the service tables were chosen, such that all sites are serviced at the latest service times. Then, we used random local search, steepest descent, simulated annealing, and tabu search to analyze the effect of advancing or postponing services on crew scheduling cost. Out of these heuristics, tabu search achieved the best results. To analyze the potential of advancing services, we compared the cost of the tabu search solutions with the cost of the benchmark solution. In our numerical experiments, the potential of advancing services was quite high, ranging between 16.78% and 24.45% of total cost.

The service routing problem introduced in this thesis implicates some open questions that provide new research possibilities. The use of a non-constant or stochastic usage rate may provide further important insights in the potential of shifting service times. It may also be interesting to consider the possibility to allow a service delivery after the latest service times, but to penalize these deliveries. Additionally, the development of an exact solution approach that provides solutions within acceptable computational effort is a further research question.

Although we are aware that there are still open questions, this thesis provides a beneficial contribution to the research of routing and scheduling problems. The service routing problem is a new valuable research direction that enables service companies to optimize service tables and service crew schedules jointly. Our solution approaches allow these companies to meet the challenge of efficient service crew planning by taking the shifting of service times into consideration and realizing high savings in crew scheduling cost.

References

T. Abdelmaguid and M. Dessouky. A genetic algorithm approach to the integrated inventory-distribution problem. *International Journal of Production Research*, 44 (21):4445–4464, 2006.

T. Achterberg. Branching rules revisited. *Operations Research Letters*, 33(1):42–54, 2005.

Y. Agarwal, K. Mathur, and H. M. Salkin. A Set-Partitioning-Based Exact Algorithm for the Vehicle Routing Problem. *Networks*, 19(7):731–749, 1989.

E. Aghezzaf, B. Raa, and H. Vanlandeghem. Modeling inventory routing problems in supply chains of high consumption products. *European Journal of Operational Research*, 169(3):1048–1063, 2006.

R. Ahuja, T. Magnanti, and J.B. Orlin. *Network Flows: Theory, Algorithms, and Applications.* Prentice-Hall, Upper Saddle River, NJ, 1993.

M. Albers. *Freight Railway Crew Scheduling –Models, Methods, and Applications.* Logos Verlag, Berlin, 2009.

J. Alegre, M. Laguna, and J. Pacheco. Optimizing the Periodic Pick-up of Raw Materials for a Manufacturer of Auto Parts. *European Journal of Operational Research*, 179(3): 736–746, 2007.

F. Alkhayyal and S. Hwang. Inventory constrained maritime routing and scheduling for multi-commodity liquid bulk, Part I: Applications and model. *European Journal of Operational Research*, 176(1):106–130, 2007.

N. Holtvogt, *The Service Routing Problem*, Edition KWV,
https://doi.org/10.1007/978-3-658-24126-1

R. Anbil, E. Gelman, B. Patty, and R. Tanga. Recent Advances in Crew-Pairing Optimization at American Airlines. *Interfaces*, 21(1):62–74, 1991.

H. Andersson, A. Hoff, M. Christiansen, G. Hasle, and A. Lø kketangen. Industrial aspects and literature survey: Combined inventory management and routing. *Computers & Operations Research*, 37(9):1515–1536, 2010.

S. Anily and J. Bramel. An asymptotic 98.5%-effective lower bound on fixed partition policies for the inventory-routing problem. *Discrete Applied Mathematics*, 145(1): 22–39, 2004.

S. Anily and A. Federgruen. One Warehouse Multiple Retailer Systems with Vehicle Routing Costs. *Management Science*, 36(1):92–114, 1990.

S. Anily and A. Federgruen. Two-Echelon Distribution Systems with Vehicle Routing Costs and Central Inventories. *Operations Research*, 41(1):37–47, 1993.

J. Antes and U. Derigs. A New Parallel Tour Construction Algorithm for the Vehicle Routing Problem with Time Windows. Technical report, Seminar für Wirtschaftsinformatik und Operations Research, Cologne, 1995.

M. Avriel. *Nonlinear Programming: Analysis and Methods*. Dover Publications, New York, NY, 2003.

A. Bachem, W. Hochstättler, and M. Malich. The simulated trading heuristic for solving vehicle routing problems. *Discrete Applied Mathematics*, 65(1-3):47–72, 1996.

B. M. Baker and J. Sheasby. Extensions to the generalised assignment heuristic for vehicle routing. *European Journal of Operational Research*, 119(1):147–157, 1999.

E. Balas and N. Christofides. A restricted Lagrangean approach to the traveling salesman problem. *Mathematical Programming*, 21(1):19–46, 1981.

R. Baldacci, E. Hadjiconstantinou, and A. Mingozzi. An Exact Algorithm for the Capacitated Vehicle Routing Problem Based on a Two-Commodity Network Flow Formulation. *Operations Research*, 52(5):723–738, 2004.

R. Baldacci, N. Christofides, and A. Mingozzi. An exact algorithm for the vehicle routing problem based on the set partitioning formulation with additional cuts. *Mathematical Programming*, 115(2):351–385, 2007.

M. Ball, L. Bodin, and R. Dial. A Matching Based Heuristic for Scheduling Mass Transit Crews and Vehicles. *Transportation Science*, 17(1):4–31, 1983.

M. O. Ball and H. Benoit-Thompson. Lagrangian Relaxation Based heuristic for the Urban Transit Crew Scheduling Problem. In *Computer-Aided Transit Scheduling. Proceedings of the Fourth International Workshop on Computer-Aided Scheduling of Public Transport, Hamburg, Germany, July 28-31, 1987*, pages 54–67. Springer US, New York, NY, 1988.

F. Barahona and R. Anbil. The volume algorithm: producing primal solutions with a subgradient method. *Mathematical Programming*, 87(3):385–399, 2000.

C. Barnhart, E. L. Johnson, R. Anbil, and L. Hatay. A column-generation technique for the long-haul crew-assignment problem. In T. A. Ciriani and R. C. Leachman, editors, *Optimization in Industry 2*, pages 7–24. John Wiley & Sons, Inc., New York, NY, 1994.

C. Barnhart, N. L. Boland, L. W. Clarke, E. L. Johnson, G. L. Nemhauser, and R. G. Shenoi. Flight String Models for Aircraft Fleeting and Routing. *Transportation Science*, 32(3):208–220, 1998a.

C. Barnhart, E. K. Johnson, G. L. Nemhauser, M. W. P. Savelsbergh, and P. H. Vance. Branch-and-Price: Column generation for solving huge integer programs. *Operations Research*, 46:316–329, 1998b.

C. Barnhart, A. M. Cohn, E. L. Johnson, D. Klabjan, and P. H. Vance. Airline Crew Scheduling. In R. W. Hall, editor, *Handbook of Transportation Science*, pages 517–560. Springer US, New York, NY, 2nd edition, 2003.

E. Beale and J. Tomlin. Special Facilities in a General Mathematical Programming System for Non-convex Problems Using Ordered Sets of Variables. *OR69 Proceedings of the Fifth International Conference on Operational Research*, pages 447–454, 1970.

J. Beasley. A tree search algorithm for the crew scheduling problem. *European Journal of Operational Research*, 94(3):517–526, 1996.

J. Bell and P. Mcmullen. Ant colony optimization techniques for the vehicle routing problem. *Advanced Engineering Informatics*, 18(1):41–48, 2004.

W. Bell, L. Dalberto, M. Fisher, A. Greenfield, R. Jaikumar, R. Mack, and P. Prutzman. Improving the Distribution of Industrial Gases with an On-Line Computerized Routing and Scheduling Optimizer. *Interfaces*, 13:4–23, 1983.

R. Bellman. *Dynamic Programming*. Princeton University Press, Princeton, NJ, 1957.

M. Bellmore and J. C. Malone. Pathology of Traveling-Salesman Subtour-Elimination Algorithms. *Operations Research*, 19(2):278–307, 1971.

M. Bellmore and G. L. Nemhauser. The Traveling Salesman Problem: A Survey. *Operations Research*, 16(3):538–558, 1968.

R. Bent and P. Van Hentenryck. A Two-Stage Hybrid Local Search for the Vehicle Routing Problem with Time Windows. *Transportation Science*, 38(4):515–530, 2004.

L. Bertazzi, G. Paletta, and M. G. Speranza. Deterministic Order-Up-To Level Policies in an Inventory Routing Problem. *Transportation Science*, 36(1):119–132, 2002.

L. Bodin, B. Golden, A. Assad, and M. Ball. Routing and Scheduling of Vehicles and Crews - The State of the Art. *Computers and Opertions Research*, 10(Special Issue): 63–212, 1983.

E. Bonomi and J.-L. Lutton. The N-City Travelling Salesman Problem: Statistical Mechanics and the Metropolis Algorithm. *SIAM Review*, 26(4):551, 1984.

O. Bräysy. Fast local searches for the vehicle routing problem with time windows. *Information System and Operations Research*, 40(10):319–330, 2002.

O. Bräysy. A Reactive Variable Neighborhood Search for the Vehicle-Routing Problem with Time Windows. *Journal on Computing*, 15(4):347–368, 2003.

O. Bräysy. A multi-start local search algorithm for the vehicle routing problem with time windows. *European Journal of Operational Research*, 159(3):586–605, 2004.

O. Bräysy and M. Gendreau. Vehicle Routing Problem with Time Windows, Part I: Route Construction and Local Search Algorithms. *Transportation Science*, 39(1): 104–118, 2005a.

O. Bräysy and M. Gendreau. Vehicle Routing Problem with Time Windows, Part II: Metaheuristics. *Transportation Science*, 39(1):119–139, 2005b.

A. Campbell, L. Clarke, A. Kleywegt, and M. Savelsbergh. The Inventory Routing Problem. In G. L. Crainic and T.G., editors, *Fleet Management and Logistics*, pages 95–113. Kluwer Academic Publishers, Boston, MA, 1998.

A. M. Campbell and M. W. P. Savelsbergh. A Decomposition Approach for the Inventory-Routing Problem. *Transportation Science*, 38(4):488–502, 2004.

A. Caprara, L. Kroon, M. Monaci, M. Peeters, and P. Toth. Passenger Railway Optimization. In G. Laporte and C. Barnhart, editors, *Handbooks in Operations Research and Management Science*, pages 129–187. Elsevier, 14th edition, 2007.

G. Carpaneto and P. Toth. Some New Branching and Bounding Criteria for the Asymmetric Travelling Salesman Problem. *Management Science*, 26(7):736–743, 1980.

G. Carpaneto, M. Dell'Amico, and P. Toth. Exact Solution of Large-Scale, Asymmetric Traveling Salesman Problems. *ACM Transactions on Mathematical Software*, 21(4): 394–409, 1995.

M. W. Carter, J. M. Farvolden, G. Laporte, and J. Xu. Solving an integrated logistics problem arising in grocery distribution. *Information System and Operations Research*, 34(4):290–307, 1996.

A. Cauchy. Méthode générale pour la résolution des systemes d'équations simultanées. *Comptes Rendus de l'Académie des Sciences Paris*, 25:536–538, 1847.

L. Cavique, C. Rego, and I. Themido. Subgraph ejection chains and tabu search for the crew scheduling problem. *Journal of the Operational Research Society*, 50(6): 608–616, 1999.

V. Cerný. Thermodynamical Approach to the Traveling Salesman Problem: An Efficient Simulation Algorithm. *Journal of Optimization Theory and Applications*, 45 (1):41–51, 1985.

C. Cervellera, V. Chen, and A. Wen. Optimization of a large-scale water reservoir network by stochastic dynamic programming with efficient state space discretization. *European Journal of Operational Research*, 171(3):1139–1151, 2006.

L. M. A. Chan, A. Federgruen, and D. Simchi-Levi. Probabilistic Analyses and Practical Algorithms for Inventory-Routing Models. *Operations Research*, 46(1):96–106, 1998.

W.-C. Chiang and R. A. Russell. Simulated annealing metaheuristics for the vehicle routing problem with time windows. *Annals of Operations Research*, 63(1):3–27, 1996.

W.-C. Chiang and R. A. Russell. A Reactive Tabu Search Metaheuristic for the Vehicle Routing Problem with Time Windows. *Journal on Computing*, 9(4):417–430, 1997.

T. W. Chien, A. Balakrishnan, and R. T. Wong. An Integrated Inventory Allocation and Vehicle Routing Problem. *Transportation Science*, 23(2):67–76, 1989.

M. Christiansen. Decomposition of a Combined Inventory and Time Constrained Ship Routing Problem. *Transportation Science*, 33(1):3–16, 1999.

N. Christofides, A. Mingozzi, and P. Toth. Exact algorithms for the vehicle routing problem, based on spanning tree and shortest path relaxations. *Mathematical Programming*, 20(1):255–282, 1981.

G. Clarke and J. W. Wright. Scheduling of Vehicles from a Central Depot to a Number of Delivery Points. *Operations Research*, 12:568–581, 1964.

J.-F. Cordeau, G. Laporte, and A. Mercier. A unified tabu search heuristic for vehicle routing problems with time windows. *Journal of the Operational Research Society*, 52(8):928–936, 2001.

J.-F. Cordeau, G. Desaulniers, J. Desrosiers, M. M. Solomon, and F. Soumis. VRP with Time Windows. In V. P. Toth and D. Vigo, editors, *The vehicle routing problem*, pages 157–193. SIAM, Philadelphia, PA, 2002.

R. Cordone and R. W. Calvo. A Heuristic for the Vehicle Routing Problem with Time Windows. *Journal of Heuristics*, 7(5):107–129, 2001.

T. Cormen, C. Leiserson, and R. Rivest. *Introduction to Algorithms.* MIT Press, Cambridge, MA, 1990.

H. Crowder, E. L. Johnson, and M. Padberg. Solving Large-Scale Zero-One Linear Programming Problems. *Operations Research*, 31(5):803–834, 1983.

F. Dammeyer and S. Voß. Dynamic tabu list management using the reverse elimination method. *Annals of Operations Research*, 41(2):29–46, 1993.

G. B. Dantzig and P. Wolfe. Decomposition Principle for Linear Programs. *Operations Research*, 8(1):101–111, 1960.

G. B. Dantzig, D. R. Fulkerson, and S. M. Johnson. Solution of a Large-Scale Traveling-Salesman Problem. *Operations Research*, 2(4):393–410, 1954.

S. Dauzere-Peres, A. Nordli, A. Olstad, K. Haugen, U. Koester, M. Per Olav, G. Teistklub, and A. Reistad. Omya Hustadmarmor Optimizes Its Supply Chain for Delivering Calcium Carbonate Slurry to European Paper Manufacturers. *Interfaces*, 37(1):39–51, 2007.

G. Desaulniers. Crew pairing at Air France. *European Journal of Operational Research*, 97(2):245–259, 1997.

G. Desaulniers, J. Desroisiers, I. Ioachim, M. M. Solomon, F. Soumis, and D. Villeneuve. A Unified Framework for Deterministic Time Constrained Vehicle Routing and Crew Scheduling Problems. In *Fleet Management and Logistics*, pages 57–93. Kluwer Academic Publishers, Boston, MA, 1998a.

G. Desaulniers, J. Desrosiers, M. Gamache, and F. Soumis. Crew scheduling in air transportation. In T. G. Crainic and G. Laporte, editors, *Fleet Management and Logistics*, pages 169–185. Kluwer Academic Publishers, Boston, MA, 1998b.

G. Desaulniers, J. Desrosiers, A. Lasry, and M. M. Solomon. Crew pairing for a regional carrier. In N. Wilson, editor, *Computer-aided transit scheduling: International workshop on computer-aided scheduling of public transport No7, volumne 471*, pages 19–41. Cambridge, MA, 1999.

M. Desrochers and F. Soumis. A reoptimization algorithm for the shortest path problem with time windows. *European Journal of Operational Research*, 35(2):242–254, 1988.

M. Desrochers, F. Soumis, and U. De. A Generalized Permanent Labelling Algorithm for the Shortest Path Problem with Time Windows. *Information System and Operations Research*, 26(3):191–212, 1985.

M. Desrochers, J. K. Lenstra, and M. W. P. Savelsbergh. A classification scheme for vehicle routing and scheduling problems. *European Journal of Operational Research*, 46(3):322–332, 1990.

J. Desrosiers, F. Soumis, and M. Desrochers. Routing with time windows by column generation. *Networks*, 14(4):545–565, 1984.

J. Desrosiers, Y. Dumas, M. M. Solomon, and F. Soumis. Time Constrained Routing and Scheduling. In M.O. Ball, T. Magnanti, C. Monma, and G. Nemhauser, editors, *Handbooks in Operations Research and Management Science*, pages 35–139. Elsevier, Amsterdam, 1995.

W. Domschke and A. Scholl. *Logistik: Rundreisen und Touren*. Oldenbourg, 5th edition, 2010.

S. E. Dreyfus and A. M. Law. *The art and theory of dynamic programming (Mathematics in Science & Engineering), Volume 130.* Academic Press Inc, 1977.

M. Dror and M. Ball. Inventory/Routing: Reduction from an Annual to a Short -Period Problem. *Naval Research Logistics*, 34(6):891–905, 1987.

M. Dror, M. Ball, and B. Golden. A computational comparison of algorithms for the inventory routing problem. *Annals of Operations Research*, 4(1):1–23, 1985.

S. Eilon, C. D. T. Watson-Gandy, and N. Christofides. Distribution Management: Mathematical Modelling and Practical Analysis. *The Statistician*, 21(1):240, 1971.

F. G. Engineer, G. L. Nemhauser, and M. W. P. Savelsbergh. Shortest Path Based Column Generation on Large Networks with Many Resource Constraints. Technical report, Georgia Tech, College of Engineering, Atlanta, GA, 2008.

O. Ergun, J. B. Orlin, and A. Steele-Feldman. Creating Very Large Scale Neighborhoods out of Smaller Ones by Compounding Moves. *Journal of Heuristics*, 12(1-2):115–140, 2006.

A. Ernst, H. Jiang, M. Krishnamoorthy, H. Nott, and D. Sier. An Integrated Optimization Model for Train Crew Management. *Annals Of Operations Research*, 108 (1/4): 211–224, 2001.

A. Ernst, H. Jiang, M. Krishnamoorthy, and D. Sier. Staff scheduling and rostering: A review of applications, methods and models. *European Journal of Operational Research*, 153(1):3–27, 2004.

M. M. Etschmaier and D. F. X. Mathaisel. Airline Scheduling: An Overview. *Transportation Science*, 19(2):127–138, 1985.

A. A. Farley. A Note on Bounding a Class of Linear Programming Problems, Including Cutting Stock Problems. *Operations Research*, 38(5):922–923, 1990.

A. Federgruen and P. Zipkin. A Combined Vehicle Routing and Inventory Allocation Problem. *Operations Research*, 32(5):1019–1037, 1984.

C.-N. Fiechter. A parallel tabu search algorithm for large traveling salesman problems. *Discrete Applied Mathematics*, 51(3):243–267, 1994.

M. Fischetti and P. Toth. An additive bounding procedure for the asymmetric travelling salesman problem. *Mathematical Programming*, 53(1-3):173–197, 1992.

M. Fischetti and P. Toth. A Polyhedral Approach to the Asymmetric Traveling Salesman Problem. *Management Science*, 43(11):1520–1536, 1997.

M. L. Fisher. Optimal Solution of Vehicle Routing Problems Using Minimum K-Trees. *Operations Research*, 42(4):626–642, 1994.

M. L. Fisher and R. Jaikumar. A generalized assignment heuristic for vehicle routing. *Networks*, 11(2):109–124, 1981.

M. L. Fisher, K. O. Jornsten, and O. B. G. Madsen. Vehicle Routing with Time Windows: Two Optimization Algorithms. *Operations Research*, 45(3):488–492, 1997.

J. J. Forrest. Mathematical Programming with a Library of Optimization Subroutines. In *ORSA/TIMS Joint National Meeting, New York (October)*, 1989.

B. A. Foster and D. M. Ryan. An Integer Programming Approach to Scheduling. *Computer Scheduling of Public Transport Urban Passenger Vehicle and Crew Scheduling*, pages 269–280, 1981.

A. M. Frieze, G. Galbiati, and F. Maffioli. On the Worst-Case Performance of Some Algorithms for the Asymmetric Traveling Salesman Problem. *Networks*, 12(1):23–39, 1982.

R. Fukasawa, H. Longo, J. Lysgaard, M. P. D. Aragão, M. Reis, E. Uchoa, and R. F. Werneck. Robust Branch-and-Cut-and-Price for the Capacitated Vehicle Routing Problem. *Mathematical Programming*, 106(3):491–511, 2005.

L. M. Gambardella, E. Taillard, and G. Agazzi. MACS-VRPTW: A Multiple Colony System For Vehicle Routing Problems With Time Windows. In *New Ideas in Optimization*, pages 63–76. McGraw-Hill, London, 1999.

B.-L. Garcia, J.-Y. Potvin, and J.-M. Rousseau. A parallel implementation of the tabu search heuristic for vehicle routing problems with time window constraints. *Computers & Operations Research*, 21(9):1025–1033, 1994.

R. S. Garfinkel. On Partitioning the Feasible Set in a Branch-and-Bound Algorithm for the Asymmetric Traveling-Salesman Problem. *Operations Research*, 21(1):340–343, 1973.

H. Gehring and J. Homberger. A Parallel Hybrid Evolutionary Metaheuristic for the Vehicle Routing Problem with Time Windows. In K. Miettinen, M. M. Mäkelä, and J. Toivanen, editors, *Proceedings of EUROGEN99-Short Course on Evolutionary Algorithms in Engineering and Computer Science*, pages 57–64. Reports of the Department of Mathematical Information Technology, No. A 2/1999, University of Jyväskylä, 1999.

M. Gendreau, A. Hertz, G. Laporte, and M. Stan. A Generalized Insertion Heuristic for the Traveling Salesman Problem with Time Windows. *Operations Research*, 46(3): 330–335, 1998.

B. Gendron and T. G. Crainic. Parallel Branch-and-Branch Algorithms: Survey and Synthesis. *Operations Research*, 42(6):1042–1066, 1994.

I. Gershkoff. Optimizing Flight Crew Schedules. *Interfaces*, 19(4):29–43, 1989.

G. Giaglis, I. Minis, A. Tatarakis, and V. Zeimpekis. Minimizing logistics risk through real-time vehicle routing and mobile technologies: Research to date and future trends. *International Journal of Physical Distribution & Logistics Management*, 34 (9):749–764, 2004.

B. E. Gillett and L. R. Miller. A Heuristic Algorithm for the Vehicle-Dispatch Problem. *Operations Research*, 22:340–349, 1974.

F. Glover. Future Paths for Integer Programming and Links to Artificial Intelligence. *Computers & Operations Research*, 13(5):533–549, 1986.

F. Glover. Tabu search: A tutorial. *Interfaces*, 20(4):74–94, 1990.

F. Glover, D. Karney, and D. Klingman. Implementation and Computational Comparisons of Primal, Dual and Primal-Dual Computer Codes for Minimum Cost Network Flow Problems. *Networks*, 4(3):191–212, 1974.

V. F. Glover and G. A. Kochenberger. *Handbook of Metaheuristics (International Series in Operations Research & Management Science)*. Springer Netherlands, 2003.

A. V. Goldberg, E. Tardos, and R. E. Tarjan. Network Flow Algorithms. In B. Korte, L. Lovasz, H. Proeme, and A. Schrijver, editors, *Paths, Flows and VLSI-Design*, pages 101–164. Springer Verlag, Berlin, Heidelberg, 1990.

B. L. Golden and C. C. Skiscim. Using Simulated Annealing to Solve Routing and Location Problems. *Naval Research Logistics Quarterly*, 33(2):261–279, 1986.

B. L. Golden, T. L. Magnanti, and H. Q. Nguyen. Implementing Vehicle Routing Algorithms. *Networks*, 7(2):113–148, 1977.

B. Gopalakrishnan and E. L. Johnson. Airline Crew Scheduling: State-of-the-Art. *Annals of Operations Research*, 140(2005):305–337, 2005.

M. Grönkvist. *The Tail Assignment Problem*. PhD thesis, Chalmers University of Technology, Göteburg, 2005.

V. Guihaire and J. Hao. Transit network design and scheduling: A global review. *Transportation Research Part A: Policy and Practice*, 42(10):1251–1273, 2008.

G. Halbach and H. Menzel, editors. *Arbeitsgesetze der Bundesrepublik Deutschland 2000*. StollfußVerlag, Bonn, 10th edition, 2000.

M. Held and R. M. Karp. The Traveling-Salesman Problem and Minimum Spanning Trees. *Operations Research*, 18(6):1138–1162, 1970.

M. Held and R. M. Karp. The Traveling-Salesman Problem and Minimum Spanning Trees: Part II. *Mathematical Programming*, 1(1):6–25, 1971.

V. Hemmelmayr, K. F. Doerner, R. F. Hartl, and M. W. P. Savelsbergh. Delivery Strategies for Blood Products Supplies. *OR Spectrum*, 31(4):707–725, 2008.

Y. Herer and R. Roundy. Heuristics for a One-Warehouse Multiretailer Distribution Problem with Performance Bounds. *Operations Research*, 45(1):102–115, 1997.

K. Hoffman and M. Padberg. Solving Airline Crew Scheduling Problems by Branch-and-Cut. *Management Science*, 39(6):657–682, 1993.

K. Hoffman and M. Padberg. Set Covering, Packing and Partitioning Problems. In C. A. Floudas and P. M. Pardalos, editors, *Encyclopedia of Optimization, Part 19*, pages 3482–3486. Springer US, Boston, MA, 2009.

J. H. Holland. *Adaptation in Natural and Artificial Systems*. The University of Michigan Press, Ann Arbor, MA, 1975.

N. Holtvogt and U. W. Thonemann. Modeling and Solving the Service Routing Problem. Working paper, Seminar for Supply Chain Management and Management, Cologne. 2011.

J. Homberger and H. Gehring. Two Evolutionary Metaheuristics for the Vehicle Routing Problem with Time Windows. *Information System and Operations Research*, 37: 297–318, 1999.

S. Irnich and G. Desaulniers. Shortest Path Problems with Resource Constraints. In Guy Desaulniers, A. Desrosiers, and M. M. Solomon, editors, *Column Generation*, pages 33–65. Springer Verlag, Berlin, Heidelberg, 2005.

P. Jaillet, J. F. Bard, L. Huang, and M. Dror. Delivery Cost Approximations for Inventory Routing Problems in a Rolling Horizon Framework. *Transportation Science*, 36(3): 292–300, 2002.

J. W. Joubert. *An integrated and intelligent metaheuristic for constrained vehicle routing*. PhD thesis, University Of Pretoria, South Africa, 2007.

P.-C. Kanellakis and C. H. Papadimitriou. Local Search for the Asymmetric Traveling Salesman Problem. *Operations Research*, 28(5):1086–1099, 1980.

R. L. Karg and G. L. Thompson. A Heuristic Approach to Solving Travelling Salesman Problems. *Management Science*, 10(2):225–248, 1964.

R. M. Karp. A Patching Algorithm for the Nonsymmetric Traveling-Salesman Problem. *SIAM Journal on Computing*, 8(4):561, 1979.

P. Kilby, P. Prosser, and P. Shaw. Guided Local Search for the Vehicle Routing Problem with Time Windows. In S. Voss, S. Martello, I. Osman, and C. Roucairol, editors, *Meta-Heuristics: Advances and Trends in Local Search Paradigms for Optimization*, pages 473–486. Kluwer Academic Publisher, Boston, MA, 1999.

S. Kirkpatrick. Optimization by Simulated Annealing: Quantitative Studies. *Journal of Statistical Physics*, 34(5-6):975–986, 1984.

S. Kirkpatrick, C. D. Gelatt, and M. P. Vecchi. Optimization by Simulated Annealing. *Science*, 220(4598):671–80, 1983.

D. Klabjan and K. Schwan. Airline Crew Pairing Generation in Parallel. In *Proceedings of the 10th SIAM Conference on Parallel Processing for Scientific Computing*, Portsmouth, VI, 2001.

D. Klabjan, E. L. Johnson, and G. L. Nemhauser. Solving Large Airline Crew Scheduling Problems : Random Pairing Generation and Strong Branching. In *Computational Optimization and Applications*, pages 73–91, 2001.

A. J. Kleywegt, V. S. Nori, and M. W. P. Savelsbergh. The Stochastic Inventory Routing Problem with Direct Deliveries. *Transportation Science*, 36(1):94–118, 2002.

A. J. Kleywegt, V. S. Nori, and M. W. P. Savelsbergh. Dynamic Programming Approximations for a Stochastic Inventory Routing Problem. *Transportation Science*, 38(1): 42–70, 2004.

J. Knox. Tabu Search Performance on the Symmetric Traveling Salesman Problem. *Computers & Operations Research*, 21(8):867–876, 1994.

N. Kohl and O. B. G. Madsen. An Optimization Algorithm for the Vehicle Routing Problem with Time Windows Based on Lagrangian Relaxation. *Operations Research*, 45(3):395–406, 1997.

A. W. J. Kolen, A. H. G. Rinnooy Kan, and H. Trienekens. Vehicle routing with time windows. *Operations research*, 35:266–273, 1987.

R. Kolisch, A. Sprecher, and A. Drexl. Characterization and Generation of a General Class of Resource-Constrained Project Scheduling Problems. *Management Science*, 41(10):1693–1703, 1995.

G. Kontoravdis and J. F. Bard. A GRASP for the Vehicle Routing Problem with Time Windows. *Journal on Computing*, 7(1):10–23, 1995.

Y. A. Koskosidis, W. B. Powell, and M. M. Solomon. An Optimization-Based Heuristic for Vehicle Routing and Scheduling with Soft Time Window Constraints. *Transportation Science*, 26(2):69–85, 1992.

J. Kytöjoki, T. Nuortio, O. Bräysy, and M. Gendreau. An efficient variable neighborhood search heuristic for very large scale vehicle routing problems. *Computers & Operations Research*, 34(9):2743–2757, 2007.

G. Laporte. The Traveling Salesman Problem: An overview of exact and approximate algorithms. *European Journal of Operational Research*, 59(2):231–247, 1992a.

G. Laporte. The Vehicle Routing Problem: An overview of exact and approximate algorithms. *European Journal of Operational Research*, 59(3):345–358, 1992b.

G. Laporte. Fifty Years of Vehicle Routing. *Transportation Science*, 43(4):408–416, 2009.

G. Laporte and Y. Nobert. A Branch and Bound Algorithm for the Capacitated Vehicle Routing Problem. *OR Spektrum*, 5(2):77–85, 1983.

J. Larsen. *Parallelization of the Vehicle Routing Problem with Time Windows*. PhD thesis, Technical University of Denmark, Copenhagen, 1999.

L. Lasdon. *Optimization Theory for Large Systems*. Dover Publications, London, 2002.

S. Lavoie, M. Minoux, and E. Odier. A new approach for crew pairing problems by column generation with an application to air transportation. *European Journal of Operational Research*, 35(1):45–58, 1988.

E. L. Lawler and D. E. Wood. Branch-and-Bound Methods: A Survey. *Operations Research*, 14(4):699–719, 1966.

J. K. Lenstra and A. H. G. R. Kan. Complexity of Vehicle Routing and Scheduling Problems. *Networks*, 11(2):221–227, 1981.

H. Li. Local search with annealing-like restarts to solve the VRPTW. *European Journal of Operational Research*, 150(1):115–127, 2003.

S. Lin. Computer Solutions of the Traveling Salesman Problem. *Bell System Technical Journal*, 44(10):2245–2269, 1965.

S. Lin and B. W. Kernighan. An Effective Heuristic Algorithm for the Traveling-Salesman Problem. *Operations Research*, 21(2):498–516, 1973.

J. T. Linderoth and M. W. P. Savelsbergh. A Computational Study of Search Strategies for Mixed Integer Programming. *Journal on Computing*, 11(2):173–187, 1999.

J. D. C. Little, K. G. Murty, D. W. Sweeney, and C. Karel. An Algorithm for the Traveling Salesman Problem. *Operations Research*, 11(6):972–989, 1963.

F. Liu. A route-neighborhood-based metaheuristic for vehicle routing problem with time windows. *European Journal of Operational Research*, 118(3):485–504, 1999.

M. E. Lübbecke and J. Desrosiers. Selected Topics in Column Generation. *Operations Research*, 53(6):1007–1023, 2005.

J. Lysgaard, A. N. Letchford, and R. W. Eglese. A new branch-and-cut algorithm for the capacitated vehicle routing problem. *Mathematical Programming*, 100(2):423–445, 2004.

D. Malcherek. *Ein modulares Column Generation Framework zur effizienten Entwicklung von Crew Scheduling Software — Konzeption - Design - Anwendungen.* Shaker Verlag, Aachen, 2010.

M. Malek, M. Guruswamy, M. Pandya, and H. Owens. Serial and Parallel Simulated Annealing and Tabu Search Algorithms for the Traveling Salesman Problem. *Annals of Operations Research*, 21(1):59–84, 1989.

S. Martello and P. Toth. A heuristic approach to the bus driver scheduling problem. *European Journal of Operational Research*, 24(1):106–117, 1986.

N. Metropolis, A. W. Rosenbluth, M. N. Rosenbluth, A. H. Teller, and E. Teller. Equation of State Calculations by Fast Computing Machines. *The Journal of Chemical Physics*, 21(6):1087, 1953.

J. C. Meza. Steepest descent. *Wiley Interdisciplinary Reviews: Computational Statistics*, 2(6):719–722, 2010.

C. E. Miller, A. W. Tucker, and R. A. Zemlin. Integer Programming Formulation of Traveling Salesman Problems. *Journal of the ACM*, 7(4):326–329, 1960.

D. L. Miller and J. F. Pekny. Exact Solution of Large Asymmetric Traveling Salesman Problems. *Science*, 251(4995):754–761, 1991.

M. Mitchell. *An introduction to genetic algorithms*. MIT Press, Cambridge, MA, 1998.

N. Mladenovic and P. Hansen. Variable Neighborhood Search. *Computers & Operations Research*, 24(11):1097–1100, 1997.

R. H. Mole and S. R. Jameson. A Sequential Route-Building Algorithm Employing a Generalised Savings Criterion. *Operational Research Quarterly*, 27:503–511, 1976.

Y. Nagata and O. Bräysy. Edge Assembly-Based Memetic Algorithm for the Capacitated Vehicle Routing Problem. *Networks*, 54(4):205–215, 2009.

S. Nahar, S. Sahni, and E. Shragowitz. Simulated Annealing and Combinatorial Optimization. In *Proceedings of the 23rd ACM/IEEE conference on Design automation - DAC '86*, pages 293–299, New York, NY, 1986. ACM Press.

K. Nurmi. Travelling Salesman Problem Tools for Microcomputers. *Computers & Operations Research*, 18(8):741–749, 1991.

I. Or. *Traveling salesman-type combinatorial problems and their relation to the logistics of regional blood banking*. PhD thesis, Northwestern University, Evanston, IL, 1976.

H. Paessens. The savings algorithm for the vehicle routing problem. *European Journal of Operational Research*, 34(3):336–344, 1988.

D. Pisinger and S. Ropke. A general heuristic for vehicle routing problems. *Computers & Operations Research*, 34(8):2403–2435, 2007.

J. Potvin and S. Bengio. The Vehicle Routing Problem with Time Windows Part II: Genetic Search. *Journal on Computing*, 8(2):165, 1996.

J.-Y. Potvin and C. Robillard. Clustering for vehicle routing with a competitive neural network. *Neurocomputing*, 8(2):125–139, 1995.

J.-Y. Potvin and J.-M. Rousseau. A parallel route building algorithm for the vehicle routing and scheduling problem with time windows. *European Journal of Operational Research*, 66(3):331–340, 1993.

J.-Y. Potvin and J.-M. Rousseau. An Exchange Heuristic for Routeing Problems with Time Windows. *The Journal of the Operational Research Society*, 46(12):1433, 1995.

J.-Y. Potvin, T. Kervahut, B.-L. Garcia, and J.-M. Rousseau. The Vehicle Routing Problem with Time Windows Part I: Tabu Search. *Journal on Computing*, 8(2):158–164, 1996.

C. Prins. A simple and effective evolutionary algorithm for the vehicle routing problem. *Computers & Operations Research*, 31(12):1985–2002, 2004.

C. Prins. A GRASP x Evolutionary Local Search Hybrid for the Vehicle Routing Problem. In F. B. Pereira and J. Tavares, editors, *Bio-inspired Algorithms for the Vehicle Routing Problem*, Studies in Computational Intelligence, pages 35–53. Springer Verlag, Berlin, Heidelberg, 2009.

W. Qiao, M. Hamedi, and A. Haghani. Algorithm for Crew-Scheduling Problem with Bin-Packing Features. *Transportation Research Record: Journal of the Transportation Research Board*, 2197(1):80–88, 2010.

W. Qu. An integrated inventory-transportation system with modified periodic policy for multiple products. *European Journal of Operational Research*, 115(2):254–269, 1999.

T. K. Ralphs, L. Ladányi, and L. E. Trotter. Branch, Cut, and Price: Sequential and Parallel. *Computational Combinatorial Optimization, Lecture Notes in Computer Science*, 2241/2001:223–260, 2001.

I. Rechenberg. *Evolutionsstrategie – Optimierung technischer Systeme nach Prinzipien der biologischen Evolution.* Frommann-Holzboog, Stuttgart, 1973.

M. Reimann. D-Ants: Savings Based Ants divide and conquer the vehicle routing problem. *Computers & Operations Research*, 31(4):563–591, 2004.

J. Renaud, F. F. Boctor, and G. Laporte. An Improved Petal Heuristic for the Vehicle Routeing Problem. *Journal of the Operational Research Society*, 47(2):329–336, 1996.

L.-M. Rousseau, M. Gendreau, and G. Pesant. Using Constraint-Based Operators to Solve the Vehicle Routing Problem with Time Windows. *Journal of Heuristics*, 8(1): 43–58, 2002.

J. Rubin. A Technique for the Solution of Massive Set Covering Problems, with Application to Airline Crew Scheduling. *Transportation Science*, 7(1):34–48, 1973.

R. A. Russell. An Effective Heuristic for the M-Tour Traveling Salesman Problem with Some Side Conditions. *Operations Research*, 25(3):517–524, 1977.

R. A. Russell. Hybrid Heuristics for the Vehicle Routing Problem with Time Windows. *Transportation Science*, 29(2):156–166, 1995.

R. Rutenbar. Simulated Annealing Algorithms: An Overview. *IEEE Circuits and Devices Magazine*, 5(1):19–26, 1989.

M. W. P. Savelsbergh. The Vehicle Routing Problem with Time Windows: Minimizing Route Duration. *Journal on Computing*, 4(2):146–154, 1992.

M. W. P. Savelsbergh. Branch-and-Price: Integer Programming with Column Generation. In C. Floudas and P. Pardalos, editors, *Encyclopedia of Optimization*, pages 218–221. Kluwer Academic Publishers, Boston, MA, 2001.

M. W. P. Savelsbergh and J. Song. Inventory routing with continuous moves. *Computers & Operations Research*, 34(6):1744–1763, 2007.

A. Scholl. Balancing and sequencing of assembly lines. Technical report, Darmstadt Technical University, Department of Business Administration, Economics and Law, Institute for Business Studies, Darmstadt, 1999.

L. B. Schwarz, J. Ward, and X. Zhai. Joint Transportation-And-Inventory Problems In Supply Chains: A Review. Working paper, Krannert School of Management, Purdue University, West Lafayette, IN. 2004.

R. Sedgewick. *Algorithms in C++, Part 5, Graph Algorithms.* Addison-Wesley Professional, Boston, MA, 2002.

R. Sharda, S. Voß, F. Glover, and R. Marti. Tabu Search. In E. Alba and R. Martí, editors, *Metaheuristic Procedures for Training Neutral Networks*, pages 53–69. Springer US, New York, NY, 2006.

J. Siek, L.-Q. Lee, and A. Lumsdaine. *The Boost Graph Library User Guide and Reference Manual.* Addison-Wesley Longman Publishing Co., Inc., Boston, MA, 2002.

M. M. Solomon. On the worst-case performance of some heuristics for the vehicle routing and scheduling problem with time window constraints. *Networks*, 16(2): 161–174, 1986.

M. M. Solomon. Algorithms for the Vehicle Routing and Scheduling Problems with Time Window Constraints. *Operations Research*, 35(2):254–265, 1987.

I. Steinzen, V. Gintner, L. Suhl, and N. Kliewer. A Time-Space Network Approach for the Integrated Vehicle- and Crew-Scheduling Problem with Multiple Depots. *Transportation Science*, 44(3):367–382, 2010.

E. D. Taillard, P. Badeau, M. Gendreau, F. Guertin, and J.-Y. Potvin. A Tabu Search Heuristic for the Vehicle Routing Problem with Soft Time Windows. *Transportation Science*, 31(2):170–186, 1997.

R. Tarjan. Depth-First Search and Linear Graph Algorithms. *SIAM Journal on Computing*, 1(2):146, 1972.

S. R. Thangiah. Vehicle Routing with Time Windows using Genetic Algorithms. In L. Chambers, editor, *Application handbook of genetic algorithms: new frontiers vol. II*, pages 253–277. CRC Press, Boca Raton, FL, 1995.

S. R. Thangiah. A Hybrid Genetic Algorithm, Simulated Annealing and Tabu Search Heuristic for Vehicle Routing Problems with Time Windows. In L. Chambers, editor, *Practical Handbook of Genetic Algorithms, Volume III: Complex Structures*, pages 347–381. CRC Press, Boca Raton, FL, 1999.

The World Bank. GNI (constant US$), Date accessed: 9th June 2011, 2011a. URL http://data.worldbank.org/indicator/NV.GNP.MKTP.KD.

The World Bank. Services, etc., value added (constant 2000 US$), Date accessed: 9th June 2011, 2011b. URL http://data.worldbank.org/indicator/NV.SRV.TETC.KD.

P. M. Thompson and J. B. Orlin. The Theory of Cyclic Transfers. Working paper, Operations Research Center, MIT, Cambridge, MA. 1989.

P. M. Thompson and H. N. Psaraftis. Cyclic Transfer Algorithm for Multivehicle Routing and Scheduling Problems. *Operations Research*, 41(5):935–946, Sept. 1993.

F. A. Tillman and T. M. Cain. An Upperbound Algorithm for the Single and Multiple Terminal Delivery Problem. *Management Science*, 18(11):664–682, 1972.

V. P. Toth and D. Vigo. An Overview of Vehicle Routing Problems. In V. P. Toth and D. Vigo, editors, *The vehicle routing problem*, pages 1–26. SIAM, Philadelphia, PA, 2002.

P. Trudeau and M. Dror. Stochastic Inventory Routing: Route Design with Stockouts and Route Failures. *Transportation Science*, 26(3):171–184, Aug. 1992.

M. Tyagi. A Practical Method for the Truck Dispatching Problem. *Journal of the Operations Research Society of Japan*, 10:76–92, 1968.

A. Van Breedam. A parametric analysis of heuristics for the vehicle routing problem with side-constraints. *European Journal of Operational Research*, 137:348–370, 2002.

P. J. M. van Laarhoven, E. H. L. Aarts, and J. K. Lenstra. Job Shop Scheduling by Simulated Annealing. *Operations Research*, 40(1):113–125, 1992.

H. Van Landeghem. A bi-criteria heuristic for the vehicle routing problem with time windows. *European Journal of Operational Research*, 36(2):217–226, 1988.

P. H. Vance, C. Barnhart, E. L. Johnson, and G. L. Nemhauser. Airline Crew Scheduling: A New Formulation and Decomposition Algorithm. *Operations Research*, 45 (2):188–200, 1997.

F. Vanderbeck. An exact algorithm for IP column generation. *Operations Research Letters*, 19(4):151–159, 1996.

F. Vanderbeck. On Dantzig-Wolfe Decomposition in Integer Programming and Ways to Perform Branching in a Branch-and-Price Algorithm. *Operations Research*, 48(1): 111–128, 2000.

S. Viswanathan and K. Mathur. Integrating Routing and Inventory Decisions in One-Warehouse Multiretailer Multiproduct Distribution Systems. *Management Science*, 43(3):294–312, 1997.

S. Voß. Dynamic tabu search strategies for the traveling purchaser problem. *Annals of Operations Research*, 63(2):253–275, 1996.

S. Voß. Meta-heuristics: The State of the Art. In A. Nareyek, editor, *Local Search for Planning and Scheduling, Lecture Notes in Computer Science*, pages 1–23. Springer Verlag, Berlin, Heidelberg, 2001.

C. Voudouris. Guided local search and its application to the traveling salesman problem. *European Journal of Operational Research*, 113(2):469–499, 1999.

C. Voudouris, E. P. Tsang, and A. Alsheddy. Guided Local Search. In M. Gendreau and J.-Y. Potvin, editors, *Handbook of Metaheuristics, International Series in Operations Research & Management Science*, International Series in Operations Research & Management Science, pages 321–361. Springer US, Boston, MA, 2010.

X. Wang. Method of Steepest Descent and its Applications. Technical report, Department of Engineering, University of Tennessee, Knoxville, TN, 2008.

P. Wark and J. Holt. A Repeated Matching Heuristic for the Vehicle Routeing Problem. *Journal of the Operational Research Society*, 45(10):1156–1167, 1994.

D. Wedelin. An algorithm for large scale 0-1 integer programming with application to airline crew scheduling. *Annals of Operations Research*, 57(1):283–301, 1995.

A. Wren and J.-M. Rousseau. Bus Driver Scheduling - An Overview. In J. Daduna, I. Branco, and J. Paixao, editors, *Proceedings of the Sixth International Workshop on Computer-Aided Scheduling of Public Transport. Lecture Notes in Economics and Mathematical Systems*, pages 173–187. Springer Verlag, Berlin, Heidelberg, 1995.

B. Yu, Z. Yang, and B. Yao. An improved ant colony optimization for vehicle routing problem. *European Journal of Operational Research*, 196(1):171–176, 2009.

Q. Zhao, S. Wang, and K. Lai. A partition approach to the inventory/routing problem. *European Journal of Operational Research*, 177(2):786–802, 2007.

MIX
Papier aus verantwortungsvollen Quellen
Paper from responsible sources
FSC® C105338
FSC
www.fsc.org

If you have any concerns about our products,
you can contact us on
ProductSafety@springernature.com

In case Publisher is established outside the EU,
the EU authorized representative is:
Springer Nature Customer Service Center GmbH
Europaplatz 3, 69115 Heidelberg, Germany

Printed by Libri Plureos GmbH
in Hamburg, Germany